A Job Worth Doing

About the Author

I was born in Hednesford in the West Midlands, and loved living in the county, racing over the fields, and jumping the brooks and streams. Then when I was eight, we moved to Shelfield to be nearer my mother's family. I started work at the age of fifteen straight from school. I married my much loved husband, Laurence, in the seventies and have two grown up daughters, three grandchildren and one great grandchild. But my pastime and interest has always been drawing and writing short stories and poems. I still love working as a care assistant.

A Job Worth Doing

Jackie Venables

A Job Worth Doing

Olympia Publishers
London

www.olympiapublishers.com
OLYMPIA PAPERBACK EDITION

A CIP catalogue record for this title is
available from the British Library.

ISBN: 978-1-84897-709-9

First Published in 2016

Olympia Publishers
60 Cannon Street
London
EC4N 6NP

Printed in Great Britain

Dedication

To my husband Laurence for leaving me alone to write. To my eldest daughter Helen, and particularly my youngest daughter, Nicola, who has always been there with help and encouragement.

Acknowledgments

Many thanks to Robin Tomkins for creating the artwork for the front cover.

Chapter 1

I had got the job. The matron of the old people's residential home had told me straight away, right after my interview. I was now a kitchen assistant. I came out of my interview with a stonking headache, totally and mentally knackered. After all for the last five or six years I had been a cleaner, cleaning flats and offices. I really enjoyed cleaning and the gang I worked with were what you called 'rough diamonds'. To survive amongst 'us cleaners' you had to have a good sense of humour, you learned to cope with all sorts, but that background didn't prepare me for my new job. I had become a 'rough diamond' myself without knowing it. Now I was the new girl. I had told my friends at my daughter's school about my new job making sure they knew I was now a kitchen assistant. My days of cleaning were over.

So here I was with my new over-all on and my triangle scarf tied around my hair. I thought I looked the 'bee's knees'. Standing now hoping the care assistants would talk to me. I waited for the cook to give me my duties. Dot was of the 'Old School', her kitchen had to be clean. She did not expect to have to help with any washing up. So she cooked and I cleaned. If she saw that I was struggling she would lend a hand but normally she just cooked.

My first day was a mad rush, I came on duty at tea time and all the residents trooped down to the dining room for their meals. The care assistants waited on and I cleared the tables, putting the washing up on my hatch. I had to wash up and sterilize every item ready for the carers to reset their tables ready for breakfast in the morning. So, did I work or did I work that day? Of course all the pots and pans that Dot had used also had to be washed and put away ready for the next day. Well, because it was my first day I wanted to impress so everything was cleaned. The oven was very large and sat on the floor so I had to climb into it to take it to pieces. Then I had the job of putting it all back together again at ten p.m. I felt I had earned my money. My head was throbbing but I did not tell anyone because I did not want to look as though I could not cope so as I stood looking about me quite happy with how the kitchen shone, one of the care assistants came up to me.

"What have you done with the steamer?" she asked.

I answered with pride "It's in the cupboard all clean and ready for the morning."

At this the carer called out to one of her friends. "You'll never guess what Jackie's gone and done? She's only gone and thrown away tomorrow's porridge!" (Dot always prepared this herself ready for breakfast; it helped her get started in the morning. The night staff just had to put a light under it.) At this point I didn't know whether to run away or make some more and hope that Dot didn't find out, but I didn't know the quantities. Just a minute ago I was feeling very pleased with myself, now I just wanted the ground to open up and swallow me whole. The care assistant just smiled and patted me on the shoulder. She must have felt sorry for me because even though she had just finished duty she raced around getting this and that with her mate while I stood and tried to remember how it was done, just in case I was daft enough to do it again. Deep down though I knew it wouldn't happen again because at that time I didn't think I would be back tomorrow. I couldn't thank my new friends enough. (In fact Lizzie and Flo became good friends and we had many a laugh about the look on my face that day).

I went home that night totally, totally knackered, feeling stupid and angry at Dot for not telling me about the porridge. Also the fact that I was a kitchen assistant not a cook's assistant. The difference was that I was still a cleaner. I went to bed after getting a lot of sympathy from my hubby, worried to death in case Dot found out. Would Lizzie and Flo tell Matron? After all there had been enough porridge there to feed fifty residents.

I awoke with my headache in place and not wanting to go to work ever again but I would not let Matron down, after all she had been so good to me giving me a chance. So at five a.m. off I went, feeling like a five year old on her second day at school. My tummy was in a terrible state, with my hand on the door of the kitchen Dot called for me.

"Oh blimey, I'm dead!" I thought.

"Hello." she said. "I'm glad we didn't work you too hard on your first day." The porridge incident wasn't mentioned for a long time. I think all the carers knew but good old Flo and Lizzie didn't tell Dot.

My second day started, it seemed to be going a little better and at least my headache went after the meeting with Dot was out the way. Dot also told me the big oven didn't have to be taken to pieces every day, once a month was enough as long as I made sure it was clean. Washing up done I went on to washing down the work surfaces with bleach. Now, the bleach was in very large containers so it had to be put into the old washing up bottles, I had filled up one bottle and was leaning over the sink ready to pop the top on the other one. It was proving to be a little difficult so I leant right over the bottle forgetting to close the top. Then (yes you've guessed it) the bleach shot up in a stream hitting me straight in the eye. I couldn't believe it I just stood over the sink holding my eye. Dot was around the other side of the kitchen, my eye was now streaming when along came Flo. She could see straight away what had happened and proceeded to help wash the bleach out of my eye. Luckily I must have closed my eye at the critical moment because the hospital wasn't needed and feeling like a complete fool I tried to make light of it. Thinking as I went on cleaning 'These people must think I'm accident prone.' Yet that is nothing further from the truth. So, once again home I went telling hubby about my day. Even I was amazed, it was so unlike me to be such a prat.

"It must be nerves." he said. I had suffered all my live with bad nerves. Once again I went to work wondering if my 'accident' had been reported to matron. I knew she would be sympathetic but I really didn't want to let her down.

Now, my third day must go better, as they say 'third time lucky', at least that's what I thought. I had by now got a good working routine on the way, consequently I seemed to have more time to chat with more of the care assistants and found out they were all smashing. I thought care assistants must be a special breed; they had total empathy with their residents' but when they had a break all their frustration came out. Thank goodness for the staff room. I was asked by the assistant cook to give her a hand with the tea. "No problem." I said. "Just point me in the right direction and tell me what you want me to do." Carol was buttering the bread for the corned beef sandwiches with fruit and cream cake if wanted. So, I went to the larder and got five tins of corned beef out ready to slice. I had opened two or three and put the key in the next and went to pull the lid off. It slipped! My thumb slid along the sharp edge nearly cutting my thumb off! Blood went everywhere, I rushed over to the sink holding it under the cold tap, I could see it wasn't as bad as I had thought but it was a nasty cut. It was then that I met Lil (she was one of the more experienced members of staff), she rushed to my aid and at this point I was getting over the shock and feeling the pain.

"Quick." Lil called. "Get a chair, she's going to faint." I felt really terrible; once again I was in trouble, now I knew everyone must have thought I was jinxed. I was beginning to think the same. This sort of thing just never happened to me. I was always in control. So, feeling sorry for myself, embarrassed and with my hand bandaged up I sat through the rest of my shift. The girls were great; they could see how I was feeling no matter what I said to them. I would never convince them that I really don't usually have accidents.

Once again I told my hubby about my day and by this time he was becoming worried. "It must be the place; perhaps it's too much for you." I knew he was trying to make me feel better but I wasn't in the mood to be a defeatist, it's just not my way.

"I'll master it if it kills me." I said as I went to bed that night. Maybe tomorrow would go better. As I drifted into sleep I wondered how I would wash up tomorrow with my thumb strapped up, a plaster wouldn't be of any use, my thumb was too sore. 'Oh well, let tomorrow take care of itself.' So I slept with my fingers crossed, this time Matron would have to be told. It would have to be reported.

I went to work the next day full of anxiety. When I entered the kitchen Dot told me Matron wanted to see me and she would send for me later on in the evening so that I could get the tea things washed up (to me that sounded like 'We'll let her do the washing up then off she goes.') I must have looked really down even Dot asked me if I was OK. Everything done, I was sent for. 'Oh blimey, Just as I was getting in to it.' I thought. So far anyhow nothing had gone wrong. I stood by the door my heart beating fast enough to start a train. I knocked and was asked to enter. Matron was sitting just looking at me as I entered. She must have sensed my fear because she looked down at the paper on her desk. I could see from where I was standing that it had my name on it.

"Sit down Jackie" she said "you look worried to death, I won't bite." So there I sat with my hands together as if in prayer inside my knees. "Now then" she said "how have your first few days gone?"

This is clever, I thought, she either knows and wants me to tell her the truth or she hasn't got a clue in which case I could drop myself well and truly in it. What do I do now? Oh well bite the bullet Jack, tell all and shame the devil. "Well Matron, it's been quite a battle to get myself a working routine sorted out so that I can get all the jobs done in time but I think I'm getting there. A few hiccups along the way help you learn." Great I thought, that sounds great, I don't know how I thought that out so quickly, still I hadn't told a fib. I waited for Matron to look up from what she had been writing.

"Good" she said, "Dot seems quite pleased with you, you are quick and don't waste time chatting when there are things to be done." I sat there smiling thinking I had gotten away with the last few days and Matron didn't know what a prat she had taken on. She went on to ask if I was happy here and of course I said I was so far. She then asked me if my thumb was on the mend.

"Yes thank you." I said as I slid it out from under the other one, thinking I had hidden it. I found out later that nothing passes Matron, she finds out about everything, sometimes even before it has even happened. Now that's the sign of a first class Matron. She never got on any body's back; as long as they were doing their job she was happy.

We had another little chat and then I got up to leave, I reached the door and Matron said. "If you do have any problems just knock on my door, I'm always available." (And she was, over the years she was one of the very best.) I turned the handle and was nearly out the room thinking it had gone well when she said "By the way Jackie, don't give the porridge another thought." I turned to try and say something but she had already gone back to her paperwork. 'Oh bum.' I smiled and closed the door behind me.

As I walked back to the kitchen no one turned a hair. I wanted to tell everyone what had happened (I'm like that, a typical Gemini, the need to communicate has sometimes been my undoing, later on in my life it has helped. I know that being a Union Steward helped me to curb my need to relate all. I became very selective in whom I imparted information to but that came later on in my life.). As the evening wore on I waited to go home to tell hubby, I think he was getting used to me coming in to tell him the next instalment of my new job.

Nothing else happened that night it went well but what I had said to Matron kept going through my mind. Matron was a very clever woman and while I thought I was being clever in my answers, she with her experience probably got to know more about me in that interview than I would ever know.

The next few weeks went without too many problems, I seemed to have got over the first 'out of character' accidents. By the third week I was feeling a little under the weather, I had got used to the backaches all washer uppers get and I had got over the fact no matter how you put your washing up gloves on or how low the water is you always get dirty water down your gloves and end up with rough hands. I even invested in some hand cream, something I never brought, that sort of thing was only for the better off types. I didn't have the money in the past for such luxuries. Now I wasn't feeling well and I noticed I also had the beginnings of a rash. Now what, I thought as I ended my shift and wanted to go home.

When I got home that night I showed my hubby. "It isn't really spots; it's just a little redder than the rest of your skin. Then again you do work with old people, in a very warm atmosphere. You never know what germs might be floating about." This made me think, at this time I was helping out at my girl's school. I helped with the school bank so I was really in the same atmosphere only with small children. They had all sorts of kiddie's ailments that I might easily take back to our elderly. I needed to get this sorted out one way or the other. I decided to speak to Matron after all I didn't really come into contact with our residents so I might be OK.

That evening before I went into the kitchen I popped into the office to get some advice. I knocked on the door and went in, once I was in I realised it was the second officer on duty. I didn't really know Pam but I had heard about her, she had the reputation of being a very happy person. She had been married and divorced and she's had a couple of boyfriends. She was about 36 and very pretty. I wasn't nervous. Pam smiled and walked towards me. "Hello Jackie, It's nice to meet you how can I help?" she offered her hand and I took it. "Please sit down." I felt at ease straight away as we both sat down.

"Well." I started "It's this rash." I had no sooner said rash when she was up, her legs pushing the chair making it scrape the floor as it slid away from her. I was amazed at her reaction. I must have been open mouthed because she smiled and realised what she had done. She then asked "Who has this rash Jackie?"

"Well I have actually Pam. It's not that bad I just need to know what the rules are? You know with me working in the kitchen. I was just thinking about infection and all that." As I was talking Pam had been edging nearer and nearer to the wall. She looked as though she was trying to hold the wall up or get through it. I wondered if this person was the full ticket. "Do you want to see it Pam?" I asked whilst pulling up my tabard. At that she almost fell over.

"No, it's OK. You just stay there and I'll get Matron over." There were papers on the floor next to her and in her mad rush to get past me to the door she very nearly fell over them, I didn't know whether to burst out laughing or feel sorry for her, in the end emotion took over and I laughed. It wasn't a titter; my laugh came out as one big "Ha Ha Ha." of which I felt terrible but couldn't control. So as Pam scurried out the door at speed, I just sat and giggled with the occasional itch because I was feeling a little warm now.

It was only two minutes before Matron came into the office, she was smiling as she entered and I wondered if Pam had told her that I had found the whole thing funny and laughed out loud. Matron looked at me and said "You look well considering you have the dreaded lurgie." we looked at each other and laughed. "Now let's have a look if you don't mind." Matron looked and seemed to think it was German measles. She advised me to go home and see my doctor, "...just in case." she said. I went home even though I didn't really want to. Hubby was there and the girls were pleased to see mommy come home early. I went to see my own doctor the next day and he confirmed it. I was put on the box for two weeks and told to stay away from the school in case I came into contact with any pregnant women. Now from seeing all sorts of people to seeing no one was rotten with nobody to talk to. The two weeks really dragged. My new working life was unsettled. Whatever next I thought surely nothing else could go wrong.

Chapter 2

By the time my rash had gone I was ready to go back to work, I was really bored, the house had been cleaned top to bottom and I'd had nothing else to do so I was ready. The day came and off I went really looking forward to seeing my new friends and catching up on how the residents were. I walked up the drive and saw a few of the residents on the first floor overlooking the entrance. It was a sunny day and the windows were open just a little. I smiled up at them and thought one of them was going to get up and give me a little wave. Instead to my horror she shouted as loud as any young person might. "Hey you, just f**k off you daft sod!" I just stood there in complete silence looking up. Then a carer quickly came to close the window and wave down to me. I didn't know whether to laugh or cry. What is it with me and this place I thought as I entered the home?

I was very embarrassed and red faced when I entered the staff room, one of the staff had noticed what had happened and came to my rescue. "Hiya Jackie, I see you have met Bella? Don't worry about her she doesn't know what she is saying or doing most of the time. It's something to do with her illness she can't control herself and she shouts at anyone. We thought she had stopped it that's why we moved her into the front lounge."

"I'm glad you let me know." I said. "I was beginning to think it was just me."

It wasn't long before Bella was at it again, I would rush to my kitchen window if I heard a fracas and would very often see some poor mother with shopping bags in hand, trying desperately to hold on to young kiddies while they pointed up to the window, where Bella was bellowing abuse. Mothers would look up in utter disgust while trying to hold hands over little ears pushing them out of earshot. I'm afraid I found it all very amusing and almost wished she would call out to some poor unsuspecting person just to liven my day up.

The next time I heard Bella it was to be her last outburst (almost). It was a sunny afternoon and the windows had been propped open to let the air circulate. Bella had been quiet for a few days so the carers had let their guard down. A visitor was making his way up the drive smiling and humming to himself, he was at ease, he looked up to the residents and waved to some of them. Bella was there as if she was just waiting for him. She looked around her making sure there was no staff around to spoil her fun and then with the window open as far as the lock would allow she saw her prey.

"Oi you, just f*****g bugger off and take that sodding daft grin with you!" she hollered and as quick as a flash she returned to her seat looking as if butter wouldn't melt. She smiled to herself; it had really made her day. The poor chap (after the shock had subsided) almost crawled to the door trying to become invisible. As quick as a flash he was through the door and leaning heavily on the door handle red faced with embarrassment. Matron had heard most of it and wasn't very happy at all. She ushered him into the office saying sympathetic words of comfort as they walked in. It wasn't long after that Bella was moved into the back lounge where she could swear to her hearts content with only the staff to hear her. Funnily enough she stopped again but she was never allowed to go back to the front lounge. Mothers were safe once again to walk by the home without having a lot of uncomfortable questions to answer from nosey little people. The new priest consequently did forgive her and visited her often.

Weeks turned into months and I had settled down to a good working relationship with staff and residents and also helped the carers wherever I could or helped in the laundry. I loved it but like all good things it wasn't to last, for me or for the carers.

Our third officer who we all got on with was leaving to start at another home as a second officer so that meant we had to wait for another third officer to be employed. Meanwhile we had a fill-in officer. She was very nice but I didn't see a lot of her.

At that time I had the job of making the tea for the officers on duty. I didn't mind the job and on one occasion I was sorting out the tray and Mrs. Hills came into the kitchen. I had seen her about doing her job but hadn't yet had the opportunity for a chat. I was deep into my work and was no way expecting her to fetch her own tray. In my fluster at having an officer in the kitchen I turned around and in a vain attempt I tried to make conversation with her. I commented on her hair and how it always seemed to look nice. I really meant it but as Flo entered the kitchen behind Mrs. Hills I could see by the look on her face that I had dropped myself in it once again. I didn't know what I had said to make Flo's shoulders to go up and down like that. Mrs. Hills just took her tray, smiled and went back to the office. I looked to Flo and she just whispered to me "She wears a wig." Great I thought I've done it again, me and my big mouth.

"But it did look good." I said to the back of Flo's head as she walked away. Mrs. Hills never said anything about the incident and neither did I, we just carried on as though nothing had been said.

After a few months Mrs. Hills left and our new third officer came, she was very nice, quite chubby and about thirty six-ish. Gloria enjoyed sitting in the staff room chatting and she encouraged us to sit with her (which we did, not wanting to seem offish with her, it became a real pain though because then we had to rush about

24

catching up on work we should have done before). This went on for a while and we were getting a little fed up with it. It was about that time that a notice went up in the staff room.

Staff meeting
Agenda – Time wasting, over running of breaks and the importance of confidentiality.

We were not happy people; this person had reported us to Matron to make herself look good. What a dog! Things were never the same after that we had somehow lost a little faith in our Matron after all she had known some of the carers a great many years. Why had she taken that dogs word for all that she said. I had to be careful what I said and that was difficult (I always expect people to be straight with me because this is how I am myself), I had never met someone so ambitious before until I met Gloria that is. She was determined to go up in the world. We found out she was still training and took it all very seriously, treading on anyone who got in her way, or who was daft enough to trust her when she said "Don't worry it won't go any further." When what she really meant was "Don't worry it won't go any further than this country." We all had to learn this and it took some carers a long time to realise it. The innocent little chats they had, got them into real trouble with the other more careful carers, thus causing a rift between all the staff (it was a case of those that could be trusted and those that could not). I had never come into contact with such a person before after all I had worked with hard cleaners who always spoke their minds and 'so what to the consequences'. I found that way much better at least you knew where you stood and who your friends were. This new atmosphere was not nice but things carried on.

Eventually most of the staff got on an even footing with only the sycophants doing their usual creeping about. Life rattled on with Gloria getting more and more disliked, Matron noticed the atmosphere but in her position couldn't really do much about it, after all she had been taken in hook line and sinker. It was also the cheery face Gloria had as she stabbed you in the back.

The home had a flat above the staff room; this was for the officers on duty to use and had to sleep in. Matron also had a house attached to the home so we could get to her in an emergency. The flat had everything you could want, a kitchen and a bedroom but the kitchen was rarely used, the officers preferred to sit in the staff room or office when on duty. The flat also had its own fire escape which led down to the back of the home, this was never used. Gloria used the flat to do all her homework; it was quiet and had all the space and privacy for her to leave her important paperwork about with no one to touch it, even though we'd have loved to have read whatever rubbish she had been writing. (As I carry on in this job I have seen all sorts of people. Some that are really suited to the job with very good communication skills and others that have the gift of being able to write down what should be happening but no idea how to put it into practice. Communication is the top skill when dealing with so many different personalities. Matron used to have that skill until she employed Gloria. Matron must have been having a bad day that day, we all agreed.)

It was the day of the summer Fete and everyone in the area looked forward to the 'Miles' Fete. We had a barbeque, a baby show and the Mayor visited (only because the Matron knew him). We would also have well known personalities appearing. Stalls were set up by our 'League of Friends' and everyone had a good time. You would usually get some little twits from the 'rough end' of the area come along and see what they could get for nothing, but they would get fed up of the staff telling them off and would soon clear off, usually with their pockets full of something but you never knew what. I'll say that for Gloria she wasn't frightened of them but Matron was careful not to make much of them playing up and that was how to deal with the so called 'low life'. But Gloria had to make a name for herself yet again. We who lived in the area knew not to make enemies with these people or you were likely to get fire alarms going off at all times of the day and night. Gloria wouldn't be told.

"Clear off!" you would hear her shouting. "And don't come back." My, she did think she was brave.

"This will all end in tears." we told Matron. The Fete went well; kiddies that had won the beauty contest were showing off their ribbons, while the mothers were going about bragging about how their child was the prettiest in the area. The Mayor would be chatting up the personality whilst we were running around trying to catch the residents who had decided it was time to go home and had preceded to make their way back to wherever it was they lived years ago. (That's where communication came in handy with a great deal of patience thrown in. That was something I had yet to learn so I left that to the carers.) I was totally amused by the whole show and waited for the frustrations to erupt in the staff room later.

It was just about that time when we realised Gloria was missing, just for a moment we were worried as she had told the 'rough types' to go away (or words to that effect). Suddenly we heard an almighty scream that echoed above the sound of the Fete and was coming from the officers flat. Some carers raced to where the sound had come from, Matron made her excuses to the Mayor and made her way to the back of the home with the Mayor following on behind. Behind him a long trail of nosey people followed just to see what the commotion was all about. Everyone loves a bit of trouble to take away with them just so they can say "Well you should have stayed, it was a right performance!"

By now everyone that had been round the front of the home enjoying the Fete was now around the back waiting for the next show. All of them chattering as they went to people they would never speak to ordinarily. A lot of nudging and tutting was going on as Matron made her way up the stairs that led the flat, nothing could be seen by us on the ground and Gloria was nowhere to be seen. Just as Matron got to the top step, Gloria appeared at the door holding what looked like some papers dripping wet, we could just see that the ink had run all over the wet pages. Gloria looked to the ground and shouted. "Who opened this bloody door?" I think she was a little angry at this point, then she carried on. "If I catch the little sod that did this I'll bloody..." at this point Matron interrupted, gathered her up and swiped her into the flat. Then the crowd all started talking at once.

"What was that she said?"

"What was in her hands?"

"It must have been very important." the Mayor decided to go up to see the Matron and he began climbing the stairs when someone called.

"Go on Mayor, sort it out!"

"It's no good asking him." someone else called "The daft old bugger can't even sort the council out. I've been waiting for new doors in my house for years!"

"Yeah!" the crowd cheered. They were getting a little fed up of waiting by now and needed something to vent their boredom. "Go on Jim, you tell him."

The Mayor was just about to turn around and answer him when someone else found their nerve and called.

"Yeah, my toilet has been blocked for months." everyone had started calling their complaints to the poor old man who was by now getting a little worried about how this was going to turn out. A couple of carers followed him up the stairs trying to protect him. The crowd moved a little closer and Bella was now up the back window adding to the excitement.

"Go on get the f*****g twit, knock his sodding block off." the little old lady was thoroughly enjoying the whole thing waving her arms and swearing like a good-un. We didn't know who phoned the police but it's surprising how fast a crowd can disperse with the sound of police cars humming up the road. When the police came round the back there was hardly any one left, just us staff having a good laugh, partly with relief and partly at the fact that Bella had managed to open the lounge window and add her two-penneth. We were however dying to know what had happened to Gloria and her paperwork, we all knew it was her homework because it was her pride and joy. The police made their way up the stairs whilst we started cleaning up and someone went to see to the residents and of course to Bella.

By the evening all was back to normal and we congregated into the staff room where Matron came down with a police officer to ask us some questions.

"Now, then." the police man started. "Did anyone see during the afternoon anything at all unusual going on around the back of the building?" Well no one had, we had all been round the front. He wrote something in his little black book and carried on.

"Well Matron told me there had been an incident with the third officer and some ruffians, now does anyone know their names or where they might live?" At this point we all waited for some twit to put their hand up to admit they knew them, no one did or at least no one was silly enough to admit it. We all knew what would happen if we gave any names and we valued our cars and jobs too much.

These yobs were known to the police but they were under age and so if the police got to them they couldn't do anything about it and they would just come back to do all sorts of damage. So we all shook our heads and I think Matron was relieved. The policeman went away mumbling something like "If you don't stand up to these yobs they will just carry on doing it until someone is really hurt." We all knew this but hoped it would not be any of us. Matron came back after letting the police out, she sat down with us and looked about her. Well at least we would be in local Newspaper. It hadn't been a good day for her.

The yobs had broken into the flat by going up the stairs inside the home and had turned the taps on in the bath putting all of Gloria's work into it. It had taken her twelve months to do it and she was still in shock. We waited for Matron to go then we all agreed it really was a terrible thing to do.

But as the saying goes "'If you spit in the air it will come down as rain.' What a day.

Chapter 3

Summer carried on in the same vein. If ever it was possible I would help the carers get the more mobile residents out onto the lawn for their tea. The residents always enjoyed it, listening to the carers as they chatted away, finding out all sorts of things and taking it back to their friends and relatives. The residents sat in their sun hats waving to passers-by while the carers and myself would try desperately to get a tan (consequently the tan would only go up to the knees so when you went to put a bathing costume on while on holiday you could always spot the care assistants because of the stripy effect on their lower legs, brown knees then above that to the bikini line white!) Still we didn't think about this as we sat, this being my first summer.

I brought myself a bicycle because I hadn't learned to drive yet. I really loved that bike and would go at 90mph down the hill to my home. Mind you I only did 5mph coming to work (not because I didn't want to come to work but because the hill was so very steep).

Anyhow on the lawn I sat with everyone, legs up chatting away, it wasn't until I tried to move that I realised I had sat too long in the same place, the front of my legs were so red (when I say red I mean RED!). I moved one leg down and then the other "Argh, pain." I called to one of the other staff as they were taking the residents back inside. One of the male residents started to giggle.

"You need some butter on that love, come here I'll do it for you."

"No thanks, it's OK." I responded quickly.

"Come here." he said grabbing the butter off one of the trays and slapping on my poor knees.

"Argh!" I shouted. The poor chap almost fell over in shock at my reaction.

"Blimey. What a carry on. When I was in the war we had much worse than that. Call that a blister? We had blisters as big as plates!" he was saying as a carer maneuvered him to the door. I'm sure he was laughing as he went. 'The little swine' I thought as I hobbled back to the hot kitchen. I now had to start cleaning up the dishes and pots and pans. The oven got left as I couldn't bend down enough to even see if needed cleaning. Sod it I thought, If Dot wants it cleaning she can do it herself. I was feeling sorry for myself now. "Why me?" I said out loud as Matron walked in.

"Now what have you been up to Jackie?" she asked.

"Nothing, nothing really, I'm fine." I felt as though I had to persuade Matron to go, so I knelt down as if to look in the oven.

"That's OK then." she said as she went. As she pottered about I kept my head in the oven and tried to look busy, occasionally tapping the inside of the oven and trying to kid Matron that I was working hard. She eventually went up the corridor. I shuffled backwards from the oven and with bum in the air and knees still bent I wondered how I was going to get into a standing position again. I started thinking that I had better get used to the floor because that's where I'd have to stay for the rest of my life. It was just too painful to move, it's funny what you think about when you're in real pain but as I knelt there with my hands going numb I spotted my sponge under the oven! I tried to lean forwards to get it but just couldn't, blast and damn it, it would have to stay there forever. I had to get off this floor somehow, obviously the carers had forgotten about me, no one cared as I knelt there on all fours in the kitchen. I decided it would be easier if I tried to roll onto my side then straighten my legs out ready to get up so I gritted my teeth and went for it.

'Ahh.' that's better I thought as I watched the blood surge back into my knees. As I straightened my legs it felt as though my knees

32

had lost all their elasticity and I was stretching something that would not stretch. I was now lying next to the oven, nearly on my back. I didn't know what to do next as every move meant bending my knees.It was then that I saw the doctor. He had been standing in the staff room watching my antics and wondering what I would do next. He couldn't have thought I was the full ticket because we hadn't yet met; there was never a need as I worked in the kitchen.

'Oh, no!' I thought. He came into the kitchen, didn't say a word just helped me up again (now I won't say this maneuver didn't hurt because it blooming well did, it was just sheer embarrassment that stopped me from shouting out.)

"Now then, what have we here?" he said as he looked at my knees. As he bent down I looked over his shoulder just in time to see Matron walking past looking in my direction. I must have had a stunned expression on my face because instead of Matron coming to see what was wrong, she scurried off. 'What did she think was going on?' I thought, 'surely not.'

"You've burnt your knees." the doctor said as he raised his head (well thank you for stating the bloody obvious, I thought as I looked at him with a stupid grin on my face). "And who put butter on them?" he carried on. He stood and waited for an answer but I was too busy concentrating on the sheer pain that was now cascading down my legs. It was the butter as it melted even more and ran down to my feet and into my shoes.

"Well Doctor it was a resident, he thought he was doing the right thing I suppose." I said. The Doctor just looked at me obviously not believing my answer and thinking 'fancy blaming a resident for being so stupid'. I knew I had said the wrong thing so at that point I decided not to say any more than was necessary.

"Come on." he said. "You need to get those knees seen to." so off into the staff room I limped. He got a spray out of his bag, I hadn't a clue what it was but it was bloody freezing cold and it took the pain away straight away.

"Thank you" I said "but can we keep this to ourselves, Matron thinks I'm mad already and this would just confirm her thoughts."

"Well." he said. "As long as you go to your own Doctor in the morning I won't let on." I sighed and went to sit down, then decided not to as a little twinge had reminded me of what I had done. So, I pottered back to the kitchen to finish my shift not looking forward to going home on my bike. I couldn't phone my husband because he couldn't leave the children. I watched the Doctor as he went up the corridor hoping he would keep his word about not telling Matron. Just then Matron came out of her office and started speaking to the Doctor, neither of them looked towards the kitchen so I thought I was safe and that he had kept his word. 'Oh well.' I thought as I carried on. A little while later Flo came into the kitchen.

"How's your knees now Jackie?" she asked and I am sure she was tittering.

"Well I am still here." I answered. "As much as you care, I could have died in here." I said as I related my tale of woe. Flo thought it was hilarious and called to Lizzie and Lil. I had to see the funny side of it really. Mind you when I saw the Doctor leaving the Matrons office later they were both wiping their eyes. I wondered if they had found it as funny.

'Another eventful day over' I thought as I looked at my bike wondering if I could just manage to sit on it and coast down the hill. Well for anyone, it is daft enough to be in this situation but take my word for it, it is better to get home really slowly than to have ten minutes of torture. I sat on my bike and put my feet on the ground, slowly pushing myself along with my feet one at a time. This wasn't too bad. 'I can cope with this.' I thought as I reached the top if the hill. Well even when you're coasting you have to move your feet off the ground at some point so off I went, gathering speed, the cold wind slapping my knees. 'Oh, God' I thought 'this is too fast!' So I put my feet on the pedals ready to brake as my poor knees cracked into position. But the motion of the pedals took my legs with them, round and round and with every turn I seemed to let out an involuntary "Oh! Oh! Oh! Oh! Oh!" going faster and faster. Eventually I slowed down and managed to take my feet off the pedals leaving them straight out to the sides (I am sure you have seen children do this when they come down a hill). Great I was in control, in agony but in control. As I neared the bottom of the hill some lights came on from a parked car, I took no notice as I went careering past until I heard someone call out. "Oi you, stop that bike." I gave a quick glance backwards and managed to stop. 'Oh, no.' I thought as the policeman walked over to me pointing to the front of the bike. "What do you think you are doing?" he asked. "No lights and riding like a two year old?" I stood there open mouthed thinking this just couldn't be happening to me. I had just started to explain when another car pulled up. It was the Doctor from the home and again he came to my rescue.

"Hello Bob, what's happened here then?" he looked at me and smiled again. "Has there been an accident?"

"No Phil, I just saw this maniac going down the hill at about ninety and we thought we needed to have a word." I looked at the Doctor and explained that I couldn't stop because it hurt my knees too much. It was then that the Doctor took over my narration to the police. I stood by my bike knowing that my husband would now be worried where I was because he hadn't wanted me to have the bike in the first place. By this time the other policeman had got out of the car and joined us. The three of them were having a good old laugh about my day. I just smiled and they came over and sympathised with me, saying "Yeah, that's happened to my wife too." All I wanted to do by now was go home and go to bed but I knew my hubby would want to know why I was so late. I only had a little way to go so the policeman decided to walk me the rest of the way leaving his mate still laughing with the Doctor.

"I'm sorry." he said as we walked. "But it's not very often we get the chance for a good laugh on our job."

"Thanks OK." I said. "I suppose it is funny but it's taking me some time to realise it.

My hubby was at the bottom of our road waiting for me with a worried look on his face. When he saw the policeman with my bike he ran to me taking the bike off him. I was so glad it was night time or I would have been the talk of the village.

"OK now?" the policeman said as he turned and made his way back to his mate. "and don't forget to put some lights on it." I could see his shoulders going up and down as he walked.

My husband looked at me and smiled. "OK what's happened now?"

"Lets get a cup of coffee and I'll tell you about it." I said as we walked up the road together.

~

Now that my bike had new lights my hubby had let me use it again and it was great to be mobile once more. As I cycled to work I enjoyed the countryside, even on windy days it was really nice to watch the horses galloping about with their young lifting their beautiful heads to the windy sky as if to say 'Look at me, I'm alive and free.' The birds twittering amongst the branches, now their young had fled, they too had time to play in the dusty flowers. The pig farm was another thing though, the smell sometimes was just too much but the pigs seemed to enjoy it, or at least they enjoyed the food that was being cooked for them. (We had waste bins at the home and they were picked up every two or three days when they were full. The chaps that usually took the waste would replace them with clean washed out ones.)

So, on I travelled to work, the hill was getting easier as I got fitter and everything was right with the world. Life in general seemed to be easier even though we had said when I had started this new job that we would save my wages every week and it would soon mount up. Well that went by the board after a few weeks and now we had got used to the extra cash and couldn't do without it. I often wondered how we had managed before on only my husband's wage.

As I reached the home I put my bike round the back and noticed that the lid was off the waste bin, so I put it back on. As I did I noticed (or thought I noticed) something moving inside the bin. I didn't take any more notice than that and went onto the kitchen. Washing up done I went to put the waste into the pig bin. I didn't notice anything straight away and replaced the lid when I suddenly saw something wriggle onto my hand. It was white and looked like a very small worm. I stood there looking at it and wondering what It was when out of the corner of my eye I saw something else move, then something else. Then I noticed that the whole bin was alive with these creatures and they had managed to wriggle out onto the floor and somehow they had climbed up the wall outside the kitchen. I stood and screamed and ran into the home calling for anyone to come and see what I had found. Matron was just coming out of the kitchen and she raced out with me, then she raced straight back in and called for anyone that wasn't too busy to come with sweeping brushes to help. I watched as Matron grabbed the nearest fire hose and pulled it through until it was all unwound, she then called for the water to be switched on. The water came on with quite a force and washed all the little worms away (I later found out they were maggots). As she proceeded to wash the walls down the carers were sweeping them down the drains (anywhere to get rid of them). As she lifted the hose a little further up the wall, the power of the water hit the wall with such force that it bounced off, straight back at her and us that that were standing next to her! We got soaked with water and the occasional escaping maggot.

So now the carers were trying to clean the place up while dancing about, trying to see if any maggots had taken a shine to them and had managed to wriggle their way into pockets and down bra's. It was horrible to see and the nightmares stayed with the poor girls that had to go and shower the wriggling maggots out of hair and undies. We eventually got rid of them and Matron, after cleaning herself up, got on the phone to the pig farmer to give him a real telling off, she seemed to think it was their fault, they probably hadn't cleaned them properly and old food in the heat had set the whole process off. The pig men came straight away and renewed the bins promising to change the bins more often in the future. We laughed about it much later on but at the time it was horrible and I never wanted to see a maggot ever again!

Summer slowly turned to autumn and the trees turned from green to orange to red. It was September, the month I always dreaded. It was the time of year whereby if anyone ever visited our house after five p.m. they would get dragged in, the doors were never open any longer than they had to be and all the windows were firmly shut. It's surprising how many people will allow themselves to be pulled into a house by their collar without screaming. Although, my family got used to 'the month of the Daddy Long Legs', and never visited after five. I hated these revolting things and never understood why god invented them. They do nothing all year then come out for one month just to frighten the be'jesus out of you.

The sink where I washed up had a fan above it and I never felt any sorrow when one got sucked in and chopped up. 'That's another one I don't have to worry about' I though. I was using the potato peeler one night standing with my back to the kitchen and wearing my nerves on the outside because of the Daddy Long Legs when some daft carer thought it would be funny if she threw a rolled up piece of paper at me. Well let's put it like this, she never did it again! I shook and cried and shouted until Matron came down and took me into the office to calm down. God how, I hated the month of September.

After that episode I usually had a couple of weeks off and stayed indoors out of the bloody daft jokers way and of course out of the way of the Daddy Long Legs.

Chapter 4

Most care assistants start this profession with a normal sense of humour, but somewhere along the way, because of the different tasks that have to be done for the residents it becomes bent a little. If this didn't happen they wouldn't be able to do their jobs at all. In a funny way it also helped the residents. Very personal things have to be done and seeing the funny side of it helps everyone deal with embarrassing situations. As the saying goes 'you have to be there'. One such incident happened to me, it was a cold November evening and I was clearing away the tea things and chatting to the carers on duty. They were telling me about one lady who had been quite poorly but she had picked up nicely and with the Matrons permission they had brought her down to the lounge to have her supper. She enjoyed being downstairs again and her family were happy to see her with the other residents. I decided to go and chat with her until the staff had the time to help her up to her room. She looked as though she had fallen asleep so I crouched down to her level. I didn't quite know what to do so I put her blanket back around her legs to make her more comfortable. As I did so I thought something didn't seem quite right, so I touched her hand hoping she was OK.

It's funny how you know but I seemed to know straight away that she had departed this life. Now, I didn't panic it was a really unusual situation I had found myself in. I didn't want to move her yet I didn't want to go and fetch someone in case I was wrong and she fell forward and hurt herself. It was at this moment of deep thought that another carer thought it would be funny if she tip toed up to me and tapped me on the shoulder, which is what she did. Well, It frightened the be'jesus out of me! I jumped up and back losing my balance and taking the carer with me, I fell back and she fell on top of me. This was embarrassing enough but when the Doctor and Matron walked in and saw us lying on the floor in front of this departed resident it didn't seem quite so funny. Once again I came into contact with the Doctor and once again I was on my back. We scrambled to our feet when Matron said in a very stern voice "I'll see you two later in my office!"

I wasn't a happy person when the other carers came and said they had only been joking, they just wanted to see my reaction. Well my reaction had shocked everyone including myself. I thought the angels were after me!

It was much later on when Matron sent for us, she had been comforting the family and sorting out the Co-op. We really had a telling off and when Matron told you off I realised you really were told off, she held nothing back. It took me a long time to forgive the carers but as they said you can't weep for everyone and most of the residents wouldn't want you to.

Working in a residential home I realised that some of the elderly see death not as we see it. Not many of them got upset about someone dying yet we would try and protect them from it, sometimes going to silly lengths to hide the fact that their next door neighbour had passed on but sometimes they knew before we did.

Carers have to have nerves of steel and if possible be able to leave any type of embarrassment at the door. If you couldn't do this straight away you soon learnt, mainly because you had to be able to help with all sorts of activities that may be happening throughout the year.

Christmas was now around the corner so of course some sort of show had to be put on for the resident's entertainment. I soon found out that the dafter you were the better the relatives like it. Most of the residents didn't bother but the officers and relatives loved to see you making a complete fool of yourself. The first year I was at the home it was suggested that we should do something that the residents would recognise and it had to be something from the television.

"Coronation Street would be a good one." someone said. So that's what we decided to put on. No one was forthcoming with a script and anyhow no one really thought they'd be able to remember the words.

"OK." one of the dafter carers said. "We'll ad-lib it all." everyone agreed thinking it would be a much better idea, I must admit I agreed at the time too. A show meeting was asked for with volunteers being volunteered, choice didn't come into it. I was volunteered to play the part of Elsie Tanner. More meetings were organised and we had a great time acting the parts whilst in the privacy of the staff room. The weeks went by and we practiced the make-up and tried on different costumes we had put together ourselves. We had a great laugh.

Christmas came before we knew it and nerves took over. The stage was just a square at the front of the lounge with spaces for the resident's wheelchairs, surrounded by chairs for the other residents and their families. The stage was set and I noshed around organising props, beer bottles on tables, chequered table cloths laid with crockery and a large mural at the back hiding the hatch where I worked. We couldn't get flying duck so one of the residents had painted some on three pieces of paper (this seemed like a good idea at the time but looked really naff when we hung them up).

The music started and out went Stan (played by Flo) and then Hilda (played by Lizzie). They proceeded to 'act' having a row when the door was supposed to be knocked and Edna should have made an entrance when a resident shouted from the back "Yeah. That sounds about right, that woman never knows how to stop an argument!" Everyone turned around to smile at the heckling chap when the door was finally knocked and Edna made her entrance. It was at this point that things got out of hand, no one quite knew when to make their entrance so we all piled onto the stage together not wanting to be left out. It was terrible! Everyone was trying to get back to the plot, residents were shouting they needed the loo, wheelchairs were being pushed back trying to make their escape, relatives were laughing out loud and us poor staff desperately trying to rescue some sort of order.

It didn't work and the show was abandoned, we were in disgust and once again Matron was not a happy person. Refreshments were handed out with the wine that was supposed to have been a toast to the cast and it was passed around without a drop touching a care assistant's lips, Matron saw to that. (It's a funny thing but out of all the shows that were ever put on, that was the one the relatives like to remember the most. I wish I could have been on that side of the stage because we couldn't see the funny side of any of it!) We learned that night that to ad lib, well you had to be fast and in complete control, it was never tried again, thank goodness.

Christmas was now out of the way and a deep drifting snow made its entrance. I only lived a few minutes away and had been asked to work over helping the carers wherever needed. It was about this time that I thought 'I can do this job'. I enjoyed talking to the residents and was able to bathe the more mobile ones. The snow stopped my bike riding so getting home was a real pain. I still hate the slush that gathers at the side of the road because most nights when I walked home in the cold, you could bet some mad driver would come and splash dirty snow all over my already red and freezing legs. I would get home looking like a drowned rat with knees stinging and feet burning with the cold. I still made it into work the next day. The staff were dropping like flies with the flu or streaming colds, but not me 'Oh, no.' I tried everything to get a slight cold so that I could have a day off without feeling like I was letting the side down. But no luck, so on I went working in the kitchen, then on the corridors doing the 'easy stuff' as the carers called it. (Now some people that visit a residential home thinks that is all a carer does, well I'm here to tell you to look a little deeper because the work they do isn't always recognised or valued, it never was and still isn't in my opinion.)

By the end of February and the beginning of March the weather was turning warmer, our residents had stayed as healthy as they could at their age but the staff had had a bad winter. One of them was still off because she had fallen in the snow and broken her arm; another had got chill blanes and was still under the Doctor whilst a few others were getting over their colds and flu. So, I was still helping out. I asked Matron if I could leave the kitchen and work as a carer, unfortunately she didn't see me as a carer saying I was too important in the kitchen. 'Great.' I felt used and really ticked off. Temporary staff was asked for and I eventually went back to the kitchen feeling a little let down. I still wanted to be a carer and knew I would make it one day, so I carried on as a cleaner until I could take my chance again. I'm afraid I wasn't very helpful to the temporary staff, sometimes being out and out rude. I knew I shouldn't have taken it out on them but I did, so that's that.

It was about that time of year that we heard there was to be a new home built down the road in the village. We also knew that our Matron was the best in the whole area so we knew that she would be asked to run the new home. Everyone was a little unsettled, hoping that she would take some of us with her.

The months went along 'as they do'; the new home was going up really fast, it looked great. Matron kept disappearing and we could tell she knew something about the home but she wouldn't let on. We all tried to keep our noses clean, the absenteeism was almost nil and most of the staff thought it would make a difference (as if Matron didn't know what was going on). We all tried to get Matron to tell us what she was going to do but she wouldn't tell, she must have been sworn to secrecy, we all agreed. Even the trusty sycophants didn't know anything. Stress was showing in the staff, no one wanted to stay here, no one wanted a new Matron and all of the staff wanted to go with her if she left, it was as simple as that. She couldn't take everyone and the new home was being built very fast.

A notice finally went up in the staff room, any staff wanting to move with Matron had to put their name on the list and they would be interviewed.

"This isn't fair." the staff moaned into their coffees in the morning. "If she doesn't know us by now what chance do we have?" By now the whole home was upset, morale was at an all-time low and Matron knew it. A lot of the older staff knew what they wanted to do, without question, they would move with Matron if possible, the names went on the list and Matron did the interviews as soon as she could. She couldn't tell them if she had been successful or not because she hadn't been told herself when the new home was opening. So, morale didn't improve, we'd heard rumours about our new Matron and they weren't good. Consequently a lot more names went on the list.

I didn't know what to do, after all this had been my first proper job and I felt secure. I knew the residents and had by now done most of the jobs within the home, and I enjoyed the familiarity of it all. I felt the stress the older staff were feeling and if they were to go, the heart of the home would go with them. It was one of the most terrible times in my working life, should I add my name to the list? I really didn't know what to do.

One cold morning our Matron walked in with this other woman and she was introduced as Mrs. Holt the new Matron. She smiled a lot and we were told she would be starting the next day, our Matron would be popping in now and again but Mrs. Holt would take over Matrons duties and any problems should be taken to her. Mrs. Holt nodded but this didn't cut any ice with us after all we had another officer that smiled a lot and look what happened to her. Gloria was hoping to go with our Matron, this was another one of my reasons for not wanting to go to the new home.

So we would see what this new smiling Mrs. Holt was like. She started the next day and some of the staff were asked to go to help with organising the new home. We seemed to be working on skeleton staff; carers were doing two or three jobs at once. Mrs. Holt didn't appreciate this at all, the staff breaks were needed now as they had never been needed before and she was always coming in and out of the staff room telling people off if they stayed in there longer than she thought they needed to. Most mornings after breakfast I cleared away and if there was any bacon left over I would make it into bacon butties for any staff that wanted it instead of throwing it into the pig bins. Mrs. Holt came into the kitchen one morning as I was doing this. I was one end of the kitchen and she was the other, she shouted right across the kitchen.

"What the hell do you think you are doing?" I was really shocked by this, even as a cleaner in the factories I have never come into contact with such behaviour, I tried to explain what I was doing and that our Matron knew about it but I was made feel as though I'd had my legs slapped. Mrs. Holt wanted to see me later in her office, I wasn't looking forward to it at all so on my way past I added my name to the list, at least this had made my mind up.

After that we weren't allowed anything from the kitchen and all scraps had to be put in the pig bins. Cook had been asked to go and see Mrs. Holt and we later found out that she had been asked to cut down on waste, the only way this was possible was for the residents to order their breakfast the day before. Now if you have ever worked in a residential home you will know that this itself causes problems because many residents can't even remember what they did the day before never mind what they ordered for breakfast. This also made another job for our already over stretched staff but it was carried out and as most staff had said caused the residents to complain continually about what they had ordered. They in turn complained to their relatives and they complained to Matron. She in turn smiled at them and did nothing.

The staff found out about complaints and morale hit rock bottom once again, we hoped the heads of homes would find out and we waited for Mrs. Holt to get her comeuppance. We waited, but Mrs. Holt knew when to smile and to whom, it seemed to work, we had no one to turn to and no one seemed to care so we plodded on regardless. We had no time to have a proper breakfast so staff would bring in their own toast and hide it in their pockets eating it whilst on the run. If any of the staff were caught eating in the corridors you could hear Mrs. Holt shouting.

"I want to see you in my office! Now!" she didn't care who was about to hear her and she didn't realise it was herself that was getting the bad name not the staff, people only felt sorry for them.

Absenteeism went through the roof and no one wanted to do any overtime, even Gloria kept her head down trying not to be on duty when Mrs. Holt was on. (It's funny really how you seem to be able to put up with such treatment and still see the funny side of it.)

Once the shock of having this woman had settled in, we would find ways to cheer each other up. Like hiding in the linen cupboard and having your toast in peace, with other staff keeping look out. I'm sure Mrs. Holt knew something was going on but she wasn't quick enough to catch us. I used to hide in the larder pretending to do a shelf clean but some of the staff found out about my hidey hole and would meet me there to have a good old chat. Even the residents knew about our secret eating places and would whisper to us. "Go an get rest gal, I'll whistle when she's about."

So life went on with us having a good laugh when someone had nearly been caught and how they got out of it with the help of the residents who would give us good excuses. The staff and the residents became very close and we knew who we could trust and who we couldn't (not because they were nasty but because they didn't really know what was going on).

Bath time with some of the residents was great because we would hear all about how someone had nearly been caught and how a particular resident had come to the rescue placing her wheelchair in front of the cupboard so Mrs. Holt wouldn't look in. Mind you sometimes this backfired on us and it was on one of these occasions that I got caught, not by Mrs. Holt however.

I had been in the larder enjoying my rubbery piece of toast; the door was ajar a little when someone closed it tight. Now I thought it was one of the carers who had seen me go in and then saw Mrs. Holt coming so thought she was doing me a favour so I sat and quietly waited for this person to free me, but all I heard was banging against the door. (I didn't know it was the delivery man unloading his cargo into the kitchen where we usually check it off from the invoice.

Today this was supposed to be my job as I was the only person on duty in the kitchen.) Ordinarily I would have called out that I was in there, but because I thought it was someone doing me favour I sat quietly. After a while I was really bothered by the whole thing and wondered just when I should admit I was in there without feeling a complete twit, when the delivery man called out to anyone who might have been there. When no one answered I heard him go further into the kitchen calling as he went. I was just about to call back when I heard Mrs. Holt.

"Oh blast," I whispered into the empty cupboard. What could I do, so I called out, "I'm in the cupboard."

The delivery man called back to Mrs. Holt that he had found me, he was now trying to move some of the boxes away from the door muttering to himself (mind you we had told him time and time again not to put the groceries next to the larder door because it made extra work for us moving it out the way). Mrs. Holt made her way into the kitchen just as I emerged from my hidey hole. She didn't say a word to me. She just looked at the delivery man and said. "I wonder sometimes about my staff you know." she gave me a look to kill and moved back into the corridor.

The delivery man said something about not wanting to get me into trouble, I agreed with him, signed his paperwork and he went on his way, tittering with the smell of rubbery toast following him out the door.

After that I made sure that if I used my larder it wasn't on delivery day. Mrs. Holt didn't mention the episode and neither did I.

Christmas was upon us yet again but there was no mention of any concerts so we didn't say anything we just didn't have the time or inclination. It was a shame for the residents but we just hadn't any enthusiasm it had all been shouted out of us. We waited for Mrs. Holt to suggest something but nothing came. Christmas was very boring and we were all very glad when Boxing Day came round. Most of the staff had been on duty all over Christmas because of the shortage so we were all tired out. Myself and other staff that had been interviewed for the new home began to feel as though Matron wasn't going to take us, so we settled down to a really horrible working life with this woman.

When Matron eventually came to the home and did some more interviews we were all very relieved and it gave us hope again. Mrs. Holt didn't like the difference Matron made just by being in the home, even the residents wouldn't let her go without grabbing her for a chat (they were also very upset at Matron leaving).

My interview didn't go too bad even though I was being interviewed to be a care assistant and at last out of the kitchen away from cleaning.

Around the end of January, Matron told the successful staff when they were to start at the new home. I hadn't been told, I was the only one left and I felt really depressed. I felt like packing the whole thing in but unfortunately we had by now got used to the money and I didn't want to go back to being skint again so I put up with all the other staff getting excited (although they did try to hide their happiness from me which I really appreciated). Mrs. Holt wasn't so nice about it she knew how much I wanted to go with Matron so she seemed determined to make my life really miserable.

Matron came to tell Mrs. Holt that after February she would have to train her new staff without the more mature staff she was taking with her. Matron came into the home through the back door one day smiling at me as she walked past, which I thought was a little heartless but I smiled and said "Hello, how's it all going?"

"Well, you'll see for yourself soon enough. Then you'd better look out because your new job will really stretch you." I just looked at her in shock and didn't say a word. Matron noticed my look and walked back to me. I was nearly in tears by now, I didn't know if she was joking or not. "Didn't Mrs. Holt tell you Jackie? I informed her a few days ago." My look told her and she came up and put her hand on my arm. "I'm sorry Jackie you must have had a terrible time, I'll go and have a word with this person. Look forward to seeing you next week at the new home."

"Thank you Matron." I said in a whisper because I couldn't talk just yet.

Chapter 5

All the new staff started the same day, we all congregated at the reception chattering away when Matron appeared.

"Good morning everyone" she said above the chatter, we all responded with differing 'good mornings'. Matron went on to explain that the new residents would be admitted the following week and the in-house training would be commencing tomorrow. Everyone was to attend the training even the more experienced carers. This went down like a ton weight for some of us, me included. Still, the excitement carried us through.

"Now that's over let me show you our new home" Matron said. We followed on still chattering and getting to know each other. It's funny how straight away we all seemed to get into little groups walking from reception up to the first unit.

All the units were named after trees and we were now in the Oak Unit which was nearest the office. Each unit had a fully fitted kitchen where we were to prepare breakfast and tea. Dinner was to be served in the main hall. Here, in the lounge the furniture consisted of two cottage suites with occasional high back chairs for the more immobile residents. The fire was gas but it looked real making the units look warm and inviting. Against the far wall there were two dining tables each with flowers arrangements and place mats. It all looked very homely which is just what Matron wanted. The bedrooms were just off the lounge with six single bedrooms and two double. Each had single beds, cabinets' wardrobes and sets of drawers, all matching and sitting on thick carpet (not at all like the old home which just had Lino in case of accidents.) It was all just perfect and we all agreed it was something to be proud of. All of the other units were very similar but with different colour schemes. Oak and Ash had Medi-Baths with showers whilst Elm and Beech had proper baths with Ambi-Lifts.

We were then invited to follow Matron down the hall where a light lunch had been prepared. There our new Rota's were handed out, which was exciting enough because we also found out if we were to be working with the new friends we had made that morning. I was working on Beech unit with 24 hours a week; it really suited me (and still does). The other new officers made their way to the Matrons table and she introduced them to us (I was very pleased to see Gloria wasn't present). Sue was the second in command; Flo was third and then came Jill. They all seemed very nice and the staff hoped that Matron had learned her lesson with Gloria and hadn't made any mistakes with the new officers.

Well I now felt like a real care assistant so with Rota in hand and training to look forward to I found out who I would be working with in the Beech team. We then made our way down to the unit to familiarize ourselves with everything and get to know each other. It was one big happy family and we all seemed to be getting on very well. To top it all I hadn't done anything wrong so far, so for me that was a bonus, I couldn't wait to tell my hubby and the girls.

~

My first day as a care assistant arrived and I stood looking at myself in the mirror. Looking good, feeling good I thought, this must be a good start, Nervous? Excited? Yes both. I really wasn't looking forward to the in-house training but I don't suppose any one was so I grabbed my coat and set off. It's no use worrying now I thought; this is what you wanted so there's no looking back.

My dyslexia was a real pain, I had struggled with it all my life but hadn't realised it and this always seemed to bring up a problem. Do you mention it? If you do people think it's some sort of excuse, if you don't you wish you had (it's a bit like using a condom, at what point do you put it on and if you don't you really, really wish you had!). These thoughts went straight out of my head as I entered the home. Jen and Carol stood waiting for me.

"Come on." they said "the tutor has been here ages, she's in the office talking to Matron, oh and you've got to go and sign in, in that book over there, something to do with fire regulations or something."

"Right" I said as I picked up the pen, "where is everyone else?"

"They're already in the hall." a voice answered over my right shoulder.

"Oh thank." I said walking very fast to catch up with my new mates.

Chairs had been set out in a half circle, two rows with the tutor at the desk in front. Jen had saved me a chair (unfortunately we were at the front because we were the last to arrive). We were told we wouldn't need any note books because literature would be given later to back up everything that was being discussed so I felt at ease. I could read up at home at my leisure. Mrs. Jones thought it would be a good idea if we informally answered some questions on what we already knew so far. Maybe it was nerves or excitement but no one wanted to call out any answers. It seemed like we had all been transported back in time to school where no one wanted to put their hands up in case they got it wrong. So, we all just sat there looking at each other.

"OK." said Mrs. Jones "we'll try it another way." This sent fear running up my back, this is just what I really didn't want, I could see the signs. "We'll just start by reading through them". (I can hear the school teacher saying it when I was young then picking me out 'swine' I always thought.) I was wrong thank goodness I thought as I pushed Jen in the back.

"I thought we were all going to have to read out loud then." I whispered.

"Yeah, me too" she sighed. We were all given a piece of paper with about twenty questions on it. This wasn't much better (Now let me explain for those who aren't as clever as us dyslexic types. We have our own way of reading and we usually have to read something three times before it starts to makes sense, obviously this takes longer. I used to skim whatever I was reading picking out the relevant words and hoping I had got the gist of it, which didn't always work.) I was nervous and I couldn't control or slow down the way I read. Most of these words were new to me and took some reading.

1. Dementia, senility? What do these words mean to you? This was the first question and I had twenty to read and answer so I raced to read them, this was a big mistake (as I was to find out later much to my cost and everyone else's gain). As I tried to read and answer every question I could feel my heart racing, panic was setting in and I couldn't seem to slow it down. Question five threw me a little but I did what the question said and jumped out of my seat shouting "Jacqueline Venables!" Well, everyone almost fell off their seats laughing whilst I stood looking about me in sheer surprise and Jen pulling at the hem of my uniform.

"Sit down," she tittered, "haven't you read question twenty?"

"No." I whispered back, still with a stupid grin on my face. I read it.

20. Disregard question five and sit quietly. 'Sod it' I thought 'I've done it again.'

Mrs. Jones now stood up and with a titter she said. "Now there's a hard lesson to learn, always read a whole questionnaire through before you answer anything."

"Yeah," I said under my breath, "thanks a bunch."

No one ever forgot my name after that because it was always liked to the sentence 'You know Jackie, the one that shouted out in training.' I sat and wondered how long it would be before Matron found out (I suppose she would have been expecting it). The rest of the mornings training went without a hitch; mind you it took me some time to get over it and I desperately needed a ciggie.

Lunch time came around and my first port of call was the staff room for a cigarette where I met a few smokers (it wasn't as taboo then as it is now). The staff room soon clouded over until you couldn't see the other side of the room. Of course the conversation got around to the twit that shouted out whilst in training but by then I didn't mind and joined in. "You rotten lot," I said "you could have warned me." Some of the girls knew Mrs. Jones and she used this questionnaire often. It had often caught out a few poor sods like me. This made me feel better but I was determined to give Mrs. Jones the guilt trip and remind her of my dyslexia and that we didn't need hoity-toity twits making us feel any worse than we already did.

We all trooped out of the staff room ready to partake in the lunch that had been prepared, leaving the staff room door open so that the smoke could evacuate the room ready for us to go back in after we had had something to eat (as any smoker will tell you, you can't have anything to eat without a good ciggie to wash it down). Clouds of smoke followed as we walked up the corridor.

Suddenly all hell broke loose, alarm bells began to go off all over the home. We all looked at each other, what the hell was happening now. We stood in shock until Matron ran down.

"Open the fecking windows you daft lot!" she shouted. We still just looked on as Matron along with the other officers raced about opening windows. As the hectic scene carried on we, with hands over our ears, followed the other carers up the corridor (at this point we all found it really funny).

"What has gone off?" we all whispered "it looks as though someone has set the fire alarms off." Not realizing it had been us in the staff room without ciggies. We could hear above our noise and the sound of the alarms the fire engines racing to our aid (so far this had been quite an exciting morning, mind you I don't think Matron thought so judging by the look on her face). We were all up the windows, waiting for the firemen to arrive, most of us giggling like a bunch of daft school girls. Three fire engines came screaming round the bend of our home, we looked on not knowing whether to move away or stay and watch as Matron went out to explain why the alarms had gone off and who was responsible. All of us smokers started to move away back to the staff room, none of us wanting to be there when the fire fighters were told it was our fault. Before we had time to get very far we were surrounded by firemen, fastening up coats as they ran up the corridor with their oxygen masks swinging in the wind. Matron stepped in as soon as they entered the home.

"I'm sorry, she yelled "but it was a false alarm, our fire alarms are too sensitive!" There was a lot of 'Oh great, I was just eating my dinner,' and 'Well I was on the loo', a bit of muttered swearing and a lot of sighing as they went back to the engine. Some of the firefighters were chatting up some of the young carers leaning up against the wall. The senior firefighters followed Matron up to the staff room to show them the alarms, obviously everything had to be checked. It took quite a long time with Matron buttering them up a bit along the way. By the time she had finished the tour two of the engines had gone back to base, leaving the third to follow up later. A couple of the carers had made dates with the firemen to see them again and consequently had on the first day got themselves reputations as fast cats. What a day!

Us smokers didn't take much notice and found our way back to the staff room to have a ciggie and talk about the carers that had chatted up the firemen (mind you there is something about our firemen that make your heart beat a little faster). After a while Matron appeared and gave us a lecture about smoking in the staff room and to make sure we kept the windows open, which she then did again because we had closed them (after all it was cold outside and we had all been up in reception with all the doors open). Once Matron had left the room Mrs. Jones called for us all to resume training.

Well that mornings events had well and truly broken the ice and questions and answers went without a hitch, everyone was calling out anything that came into their heads (it's a pity the alarms hadn't gone off in the morning before my incident). At the end of the days training we made our way back to the reception, checking our Rota's and calling to the other Beech' staff 'see you tomorrow.' As we walked up the drive I could see my hubby and children waiting for me so I couldn't stand and chat to the girls. I got into the car sighing as I did so, I couldn't wait to tell them how my day had gone. There was a lot of giggling from my girls but Ven was beginning to wonder just what I had entered into.

"Are you sure you're working with people that know what they're doing?" he asked. I think his caution was my fault because on the way home I had related the day to him and was also wondering this myself. Still the saying goes 'tomorrow is another day' and I was looking forward to it.

After the first couple of days training everything settled down and the rest of the week went well. We were informed that the rest of the in-house training was going to carry on throughout the year. We were all relieved to hear it because we didn't realise how much you needed to know when caring for the elderly.

The following week we were to be welcoming our new residents and we wanted everything to be just right. Beech Unit had a large bathroom with a very large bath to match; we also had an Ambi-lift to assist us in getting resident in and out of the bath. The Ambi-lift took a bit of getting used to, the resident would sit on the seat and an arm rest would come down to give them something to hold on to and keep them in their seat so they wouldn't fall or try to get off, It looked like a loo seat for obvious reasons. You then turned the handle at the back; this would lift them high enough to get them over the bath where you then lowered them into the water, obviously checking the temperature first (I have never come across anyone that doesn't like this equipment it allowed some of our more immobile resident to have a bath for the first time in years so it wasn't getting them in that was a problem; it was getting them back out again)!

As a care assistant I soon realised you had to cultivate an unusual sense of humour and the sooner you did this the better for everyone. I had never seen anyone 'old' naked before so I must admit I wasn't looking forward to it. The best way to overcome this was to talk to the residents while bathing them, this helped them out as they were a bit embarrassed and it also covered up your own embarrassment too.

I was looking forward to my weekend off ready for our incoming residents as the home was still empty. We decided to have just one last try again with all the equipment (after all practice makes perfect). I put Jen on the Ambi-lift and went through the motions of bathing

59

her, (obviously fully clothed and improvising the whole thing) then it was my turn. Now if you've never sat on an Ambi-lift let me tell you it's quite an experience and I must admit I didn't like being in someone else's control. What made it worse was that Jen decided to take me for a walk around the home popping into all the units while I was still up in the air! I had no way of getting off this thing other than breaking my neck by jumping off and I didn't intend to try that one. So, I just sat there and enjoyed the ride with Jen zig-zagging up the corridor (because these Ambi-lifts and not made for going distances). 'Bang' into the corridor, 'bang' again into the main hall door; 'bump' as we entered Ash Unit. The staff on Ash unit always ready for a bit of fun (usually at my expense). My legs were swinging about as I was shouting for them to put me down but the more I protested the worse they got. Ash Unit phoned Oak and they in turn phoned Elm. Now there were eight carers all laughing at me stuck in the air. Well at some point this must have got boring because the next thing I knew the water was being run!

"Ha, ha," they shouted, "lets pop her in the bath."

"Oh, no you flipping well don't (or words to that effect)" I shouted back. I was getting worried by now because I wouldn't put anything past them in this state. 'Great' I thought as I was pushed toward a now very foamy bath with steam rising into the humour filled corridor. Well, once I was over the bath I was slowly lowered into it. Well there was absolutely nothing I could do but sit and hold my temper because mine by now was ready to blow, even though I was laughing along with the rest. "Just wait until I get off this you blinkin' rotten lot!" I shouted. Just then footsteps were heard along the corridor and as if by magic my good friends vanished without a trace. I sat there in complete silence with my feet just touching the bubbles hoping that whoever it was would walk past the bathroom. The steam was making my face hot and sticky as though I was in a sauna. The door burst open and some total stranger (male might I add) asked "Have you seen my mate love?"

"Erm no." I answered.

"Ok" he said and turned without another glance and closed the door. Oh what must I have looked like to him? Probably like some mad woman sitting in a chair 'in the air' with sweat running down my face carrying mascara with it, my hair all either stuck to my face or sticking up in all directions! I signed and slumped in the chair that held me captive.

"Oh come on you bloody lot" I bellowed "get me off this thing." One by one, they came back in, in fits of laughter.

"Ha, ha" someone said "did you see that poor chaps face?"

"I don't think he could believe what he had seen" someone else said "mind you did you notice he went straight into our staff room, cheeky twit." I was eventually lowered to the floor and was allowed to have a cool wash. It was time to go home.

"Oh well that's the end of our fun" everyone agreed as we walked up to reception.

"Don't ever expect me to get on that thing again" I said to anyone who was listening.

Our second officer came out of the office "Well girls are you all ready for next week?" she asked "we have an amputee called Will and another chap called Eric coming onto your unit Jackie" she continued "and they hate the very sight of each other, so boxing gloves on!" Everyone looked at Jen and I.

"Sue, after today I can cope with anything" I answered smiling to the rest of the team. Sue didn't ask and we didn't volunteer an explanation, we just tittered as we walked up the drive.

Chapter 6

Monday came around very quickly and I must admit I was hoping my training would be useful when dealing with our new residents. We congregated at reception for our reports. Ash was having two women residents and Oak was having our first married couple. Elm staff were to help with the settling in because their residents wouldn't be arriving until the afternoon.

Will and Eric came just after ten, they had had their breakfast at the other home and were being relocated because the home they were in before was being turned into a day care centre. Matron had taken the decision to keep them together for company even though they didn't get on. It gave them something else to think about other than the new surroundings. Matron said a big move at their time of life could be quite life threatening, we bowed to her experience and it wasn't until years later that I realised just how right she was.

Eric had lost his leg years ago consequently he coped surprisingly well, even to the point of getting himself in and out of the bath unaided. He really was a lovely man with lovely manners. Will had been a grafter and you could tell by the way he talked, he was gruff and straight to the point so straight away I liked him. He walked with a stick which he would wield like a battle sword at times, especially if Eric upset him and Eric could upset him just by being in the same room.

Jen and I welcomed them in and I took Eric to see his room while Jen showed Will to his. Their rooms were at opposite ends of the corridor 'just in case' Matron had said. Once we had done a tour of the unit showing each where the emergency pulleys were, Jen and I busied ourselves getting things ready for dinner leaving the men to their own devices. We were surprised to find they were chatting away quite nicely and wondered what all the fuss had been about. It proved to be the calm before the storm!

For two days the peace reigned until we were to have another two residents. They were sisters Kate and Elsie; one was touching ninety while the other was a sprightly eighty one. Kate had difficulty walking and used a Zimmer whilst Elsie thought she had only come to us to be with her sister, consequently she had great difficulty asking for help or accepting it.

"Don't bother with me" she would say "I'm quite alright, it's my sister that needs the help." This posed as quite a problem as we got to know Elsie better as she seemed to think that if she didn't need help we would have more time for her sister, they were inseparable. Bath days had to be on the same day, hair appointments, Doctors, anything that needed doing Elsie had to be there. It was really sweet to see them, Elsie kept Kate going and Kate gave Elsie a purpose in life. Elsie sometimes complained terribly about her sister but when she did we knew she didn't really mean it. It was just because occasionally Elsie was tired and needed a rest but this was difficult to manage.

On the day they arrived Eric was already in the lounge so he met the sisters first, well this really ticked Will off for no other reason except that he wanted to be one step in front of Eric (typical men, we thought). Dinner time was eventful as Eric and Will usually sat on the same table (it was silly to set two tables one for each of them) but as soon as Kate and Elsie went to sit down Will bellowed "Don't put me by that bloody hopping sod!"

"Hey now then," We started to answer back for Eric but the bickering continued.

"That's it take his side" Will shouted again "nothing changes." At this point Jen looked at me and I did the same. How did we manage to get into this, this ploy had been used many times before by Will and on occasion by Eric if he managed to get it in first (that's how Will came to move himself away from Eric).

We sat the ladies down trying to settle them in, after all they hadn't come into contact with their behaviour before. "We'll tell our Josie if she visits this afternoon." They whispered to each other. This was the first resident to find fault in the home. Of course they didn't care that we were all new to the job and that we were in fact all very proud to be here and expected everyone else to be the same. We didn't take into consideration the fact that our elderly had seen it all before and nothing impressed them no matter what we did for them. Oh well dinner time passed without any more trouble but Jen and I were on our guard ready to step in and deal with these two argumentative males.

We didn't meet Kate's daughter Josie as Jen and I had gone off duty but we reported what had happened that dinner time. So Carol and Sylv had to explain what had happened to our new relative, thank goodness she was sympathetic to the situation putting our minds at rest. We were glad she had been told of the situation before she had gone to visit her mom and aunt. This was a good lesson learned by us, always to put the relatives in the picture if there was any kind of problem, it always helped to have a good rapport with the relatives. There were times that we needed information from them; after all they knew them better than anyone. Carol and Sylv hadn't any problems with our new residents and they'd had a good sleep in their new room. They had been very pleased that they had a double room and were often heard to be chatting until very late into the evening. So at least we had two happy residents and I began to think that even Eric and Will were happy in their own little way.

Residents filtered into our new home, the relatives that bought them made themselves known to the other resident and to the staff. All this coming and going made the home feel very friendly and accessible. The unit had now taken on just what Matron had intended, a homely and friendly atmosphere. Even Eric and Will seemed to find their niche, on the odd occasion Will would call Eric names in front of the residents and we would have to read them the riot act when the relatives had gone (mind you this didn't seem to make the slightest bit of difference). Our unit was now full, Ada had been the last to be admitted and she had to share a room with Freda, both had been recently widowed so they found comfort in their new found friendship. There was also Lena, she was a really lovely lady and had quite a few tales to tell. She had come from the fair and according to the season had many visitors. Miss Trent came into the home with her budgie and niece. She was real Miss and insisted on being called Miss Trent at all times (her first name was Florence but we only used it if she wasn't about) even the other residents called her Miss Trent, usually just to prove a point, it just went over her head though as she didn't seem to have a very good sense of humour (she could be a very funny lady in a dry sort of way). She made friends with Lena which really surprised us all as they had come from such different backgrounds. Lucy and Vida were our wheelchair cases and needed total care, both in their eighties and both a little deaf but with a vicious sense of humour. They thought nothing of using the emergency alarms just to call the staff and get them to take messages back and forth. Matron wasn't very happy about this because every alarm had to be answered and at night when there was only two staff on duty to cover the whole home it was bit too much. Still, everyone got on well and the relatives were always eager to help with any fetes or concerts we put on and slowly found their own way. Breakfast was always a mad dash, everyone seemed to want to get up at the same time without a thought for us poor staff that had to cook full breakfasts. I found a way to deal with this and used to come on duty half hour early so that I could get the bacon in the oven. By the time we'd had the report and returned to the unit all we had to do was turn the oven down, the eggs only took a moment and the tomatoes or beans were on the hob. This gave Jen and I more time to see Lucy and Vida and by the time we had washed and dressed and done everything that was needed the other residents had got themselves up and were waiting for their breakfast. This worked well even though I was giving half an hour when I was on duty in the mornings. I really didn't mind because it suited me and the residents. Once everyone was up one of us would stay in the kitchen and dish up breakfast whilst the other one stripped and made beds. When everyone had had their breakfast and was comfortable we had ours. This was our ten minute break which usually ended up being twenty. We worked hard making sure everything had been washed and cleaned and we took a great deal of pride in the Beech Unit and we all agreed it was the best.

Carol had a great idea about how we could make money for the unit, she suggested making some rice wine, she knew how to make it but it needed a lot of work, this is where we involved Eric and Will and they loved it! Sitting in the linen cupboard stirring the wine out of Matrons way, she hadn't been told of our plans and we didn't think it was important; after all it was for the resident's outings.

Miss Trent and her budgie didn't care much for the smell that was coming from the linen cupboard, when Eric was in there she didn't really know what was going on, she thought poor Eric was a secret drinker and he hid his liquor in there. Poor old Eric, one minute he was sitting there stirring away and the next minute he was being summoned to Matrons office. She had sent for him without us knowing, Miss Trent had taken it upon herself to report the poor chap. Well Eric found himself in a really tricky situation because he didn't want to get us into trouble if he told matron about our illicit booze, we appreciated Eric's loyalty but it only made matters worse. By the time Matron had finished her little chat with Eric we looked like some sort of undercover liquor smugglers.

Matron wanted to see all of the staff on Beech as soon as possible. Eric had come back and was getting himself in a right old state about it and tried to tell us what had gone on, meanwhile Will overheard and thought Eric had squealed on us. Will then decided to be our backer and took it upon himself to have his own meeting with Matron and try and put her straight on a few things. So with Will and Eric going on and Miss Trent enjoying the whole thing (occasionally adding her two-penneth) word got round and the relatives soon got to hear about the rice wine. Well, they thought it was good idea too so they added their little bit trying to get us out of the mess. By the time we got to our meeting with Matron she was not happy. We entered the office with heads bowed looking very sorry for ourselves. Matron just looked up and said in her most obviously controlled voice.

"Well?" there was a lot of nudging and shuffling of feet when Carol at last started.

"It was all my doing Matron" she said. At that we all found our voices.

"No, no Carol" someone butted in "we all thought it would be a good idea ready for Christmas, you know save money by making our own wine instead of buying it."

"We didn't think it would cause so much trouble." I said "the residents thought it was a good idea too and it gave Will and Eric something to do without arguing so we all agreed it sounded good."

"Yes" Matron butted in "but Will and Eric thought they were doing something illegal and they really thought that you would be going to prison. I can't believe you all had a hand in it."

"Yes, but Matron we make wine at home and that's ok."

"Yes there's no denying that and it would have been a good idea if you'd have made it at your own home but ladies, to make it in the linen cupboard with the residents helping! Well I can't believe all the trouble you've caused. Just get rid of it!"

We all looked at each other.

"But Matron its ready to go in the bottles" someone said "we could do it this afternoon." Matron just gave us one of her looks, that was all we needed so we backed away mumbling as we went (mind you as we closed the office door we thought we heard her titter).

We ambled back to the unit moaning about how on earth we were going to move all the wine, there must have been about five gallons if there was a pint and we weren't happy with Miss Trent. Eric and Will were waiting for us as we entered the unit.

"You alright?" Will asked.

"You haven't had the sack have you?" Eric carried on; both of them looking really worried.

"No were ok, but we do have to get rid of our wine" we said loud enough for Miss Trent to hear and she looked up.

"I'm really sorry girls" she said "I really thought I was helping Will and Eric, I thought they had a problem with their drinking".

"Oh charming" Will shouted "now if it had been only Eric I might have let you off, but I have never had a problem with booze."

"Oh yeah, that's not what I've heard." The shouting and bawling ensued meanwhile Miss Trent was trying to get our attention as we tried to separate Will and Eric.

"Excuse me, excuse me" she called "I think I know how we can save the wine.

"Oh yeah, what do you know?" Will called over his shoulder "you started this whole mess you daft old sod."

Well this really upset Miss Trent who was already feeling pretty bad about the whole situation and really wanted to make amends. We went over to Miss Trent trying to ignore the squabbling males.

"It really doesn't matter" we said holding her hand.

"Oh yes it does." she said quite forcefully. "Now if we call my niece and she comes in we can get all that wine bottled this afternoon and she could save it at her house, she owes me a favour."

"Well Matron did say get rid of it, she didn't exactly say throw it away." we said to each other.

"No, no we couldn't expect you to do that Miss Trent" we said without real feeling and really hoping she would go and phone Karen.

"I'll do it" she said "I'll phone her straight away and she can come and help us". We didn't try and stop her and said that if she agreed we would all help but if she said no we would throw it all away. If Matron found out we would all be in deep trouble. Miss Trent returned smiling

"She is on her way."

We all shot into the linen cupboard, Will and Eric grabbed the funnel and we got stuck into it. It took some time but we managed to get the wine bottled up, the smell was really bad. Miss Trent was really enjoying herself, corks, crates and residents all helping.

"I only hope it tastes all right by the time Christmas comes around" we all agreed. It took a few trips back and forth to Karen's car before we were all done. Luckily Matron didn't bother us, we thought she might have secretly known what was going on but decided to look the other way.

By late afternoon we all sat with the residents and had a good laugh about the spillages and trip ups we'd had throughout the day. We were all really on tenter-hooks in case Matron came down so we agreed we'd all had enough that day. The residents went to bed and we all went home leaving the unit smelling like a brewery (it took ages for the smell to go away).

Matron came down the next day to see if all the wine had gone, she was sorry that it all had to be discarded but rules were rules and warned us never to do anything like that again.

Will and Eric sat together having a good old laugh at what Matron was saying and Miss Trent sat chatting to her budgie. Ada and Freda sat with their heads together and all you could hear was "Yes my husband used to enjoy his wine too."

"Oh yes so did mine" they looked at Matron and smiled "hello Matron and how are you today?" We were all sure Matron had caught on but she had looked around the unit and found nothing so she really didn't know what the happy atmosphere was all about. She didn't ask any questions and shaking her head she went back to the office. Our unit became very close and every time Karen came to visit her aunt she was the centre of attention as everyone asked about the wine. Everyone was looking forward to Christmas to taste it!

Chapter 7

Autumn turned to winter so very quickly, the local children had frightened everyone with their fireworks and Guy Fawkes. We all enjoyed the fun especially when someone said that the Guy looked like our Eric. Children can be cruel without realizing it but Will made sure to tell everyone afterwards.

"Yeah, those kids were great, a one legged Guy Fawkes they had done, the little buggers." And he made sure he was looking at Eric when he said it.

"Yeah" said Eric "and I bet I know who put them up to it you rotten old swine."

"Off they go again" Miss Trent said to her budgie. Carol and I turned quickly and scurried off up the corridor biting our knuckles as we went in a vain attempt to stop ourselves from laughing out loud. The situation was really funny (you had to be there) and we wouldn't put it past our trouble making Will either.

Carol by now had made a start on four Christmas cakes, two for the home and two for herself.

"Well" she would say "you always buy too many ingredients and I might as well bake my own cakes while I'm making these ones." Matron knew about the two raffle cakes but not the ones she was making for herself and no one was going to say anything because Carol made a smashing cake and we all hoped to win one.

We decided to have a unit meeting with all the staff residents and relatives. We turned it into a coffee evening to make it more relaxed with a curry supper. It turned into a really good party and we had said that if the relatives wanted to bring a bottle we wouldn't stop them, it was their families' home and we encouraged them to treat it as such. Word went around that everyone was bringing a bottle meanwhile our notices went up saying 'Come to the coffee evening and get involved in our plans for Christmas'. Everyone wanted to come and our unit was fast getting the reputation as the unit to be in, I don't know why. Carol as usual made the curry and there was enough to feed all the home and it was a good job because we all had to have something to soak up the wine that the relatives had 'surprisingly' brought with them. I think Matron knew what was going on (probably because we had borrowed all the glasses from the other units, just in case you understand). Karen had smuggled in 3 bottles of rice wine which our residents made sure to try before the evening started. Will and Eric were sitting by the window with a bottle of rice wine between them, acting as though they were real connoisseurs. At least for tonight they were getting on. One of carols cakes was to be raffled off along with all sorts of Christmas odds and ends people had donated. It's surprising how a little rice wine and curry will loosen people's pockets. Financially we made quite a bit and managed to plan Christmas. Our relatives were the best in the home we all agreed and Christmas was going to be a lovely time.

Matron had decided a Christmas concert would be the best idea for our first year at The Spinney. She wanted to invite as many important people as she knew. There had been a staff meeting to discuss what we were going to put on and of course Beech Unit had already decided with the help of the relatives. Matron was impressed and made sure all the other Units were going to contribute as much effort. Josie, Katie's daughter had asked if she could involve her daughter's choir and they would all sing 'A Partridge in A Pear Tree'. We were over the moon and all the residents were enthusiastic so we organised our first concert over yet another 'coffee' evening (again without Matron's knowledge of the added 'bring a bottle').

72

Katie's choir was to stand at the back of the residents with the staff standing next to anyone who wanted to take part, just to give them a hand. Each resident had a large piece of card and on each would be drawn a partridge, two turtle doves and so on. Where appropriate they would hold up the card ready for everyone to join in the singing. I had drawn the short straw and had the 'five gold rings' bit to sing with (of all people) Will. Will couldn't sing a note but was so loud it drowned out his awful voice. Vicky, Sylv and Jen had the job of drawing all the pictures which became a mad race because in our enthused state we thought it would be easy to do, but in fact it was really, really difficult. We were confident (at least to Matron) that we would be ready in time for the concert.

We had rehearsals and yet more 'coffee' evenings, which turned into 'get-togethers' with a good laugh for good measure. All the other units were really lagging in their ideas, but we didn't care, our bit was going to be fine. Ash unit had decided to have auditions amongst their residents and finally they found two really nice singers that were going to do 'There's a hole in my bucket' with props and costumes. Oak unit were going to sing a few of the more know carols and Elm had two residents who could play the organ and mouth organ, so at last we all knew what we were doing. Matron was very pleased with her new staff and really made us feel good about ourselves. It's always nice to get a pat on the back now and again.

Matron asked for one last meeting with if possible a full dress rehearsal with no audience. (Now if you have ever had the chance to stand and sing in front of any of your friends you will know that Matron was wrong, we really should have had a small audience, it does make a difference but we didn't know this at the time and excitement carried us through). The rehearsal went really well and we all came away feeling great with everyone full of excitement and confidence (we could take this concert around all the homes, ones that hadn't got a Matron with so much confidence in them). We decided on a date just after Christmas so that everyone could attend, before Christmas was just too busy for everyone.

So, on the twenty ninth of December at seven p.m. Beech unit stood in front of about one hundred and fifty guests (some of whom were very important – at least to Matron). Were we nervous? Yes, we were!

Each of the residents had a care assistant close by ready to prompt them if they needed it, I stood between Eric and Will and they had been behaving themselves all day. Karen had brought in another three bottles of our rice wine and we hadn't been told so when Eric looked at Will with a strange look in his eye I really should have known that things weren't going to go as planned. I noticed the look and straight away gave Carol a prod in front of me. Just as the music started, Will took out the rice wine and for all to see had a good sip from it. Matron looked directly at me, I quickly looked away but I knew that look and dread entered my whole body. "Oh bugger" I whispered with my head bent. Mine and Will's prompt came and I nudged Will to hold his card up with five gold rings on it. The singing rang out even though you could hear Will's bellowing voice over everyone else's. We carried on with my voice being slowly drowned out by Will, who consequently by now was really enjoying himself after having a few more crafty swigs from the bottle. He became more and more confident and eventually Wills voice bellowed out throughout all of the verses. No one realised just how one mans slurred voice could go on and on and how a 'Partridge in a Pear Tree' could sound so blinkin terrible. It seemed to go on forever especially when you wanted it to stop. We eventually came to the end and Will was truly pie-eyed. Eric was really annoyed with him and Josie's friends quickly left without hearing the rest of the songs. Matron looked as though she was going to burst with something, so we all scurried off helping Will down the corridor wondering if we needed a Doctor.

All the other residents really enjoyed the whole thing, not knowing what had gone on; most of them were a little hard of hearing anyway so they really hadn't heard the full content of Will's singing. We did get a really good applause at the end and even the VIP's were smiling and clapping. We were too annoyed with Will to really hear anything. Once back on the unit we sorted out the residents that wanted to be back for the party and put to bed the ones that were too tired. Back in the hall we circulated and chatted with other staff and we made sure to give Matron a wide birth. Six of us were asked to see Matron the next day and we were nervous. Would this be a really good telling off or a verbal warning. We really didn't know, we did know however that Will had spoiled our first Christmas and he wouldn't be trusted again. He had been very sorry for himself that morning and we made sure to tell him that we had to go and see Matron that day. Eric looked really smug and made sure to rub Will up the wrong way all morning. As we stood by the office door we could hear other voices. Oh God, we thought, that's it, it's the sack for us all for sure. Then before we were called in we heard a roar of laughter.

"Enter" Matron called from inside the office. We looked at each other and went in with heads bowed and hands behind our backs. On entering we could see Matrons expression was blank so we couldn't see what sort of mood she was in. She sat at her desk with three men and a woman, we hadn't a clue who they were and by the time we all congregated in the office it was packed. The door was firmly shut and one of the men looked in our direction and started.

"It was your unit was it that had the idea to put on a show for the residents at Christmas?"

"Yes that's right" I thought I should answer.

Then the woman spoke "It's as I have always said about you Matron."

At this we all thought we had got Matron into trouble too and as if someone had flicked a switch we all started "Now hang on a moment, it has nothing to do with Matron" one of us said "she knew nothing about it."

Matron looked up and started twitching, the women carried on speaking.

"Oh it's all right, Matron's not in any trouble, in fact we all agreed it was the best nights entertainment we've had in a long time." She said "Even the little chap pretending to be a little worse for wear was just brilliant. We really do want to see him afterwards."

Well the sigh of relief hit the electric air and we all smiled together nudging each other and giggling with relief. After that the meeting went really well and we all had a pat on the back with matron saying as we left the office.

"I'll see you later, now will one of you send Will up if he isn't doing anything. Thank you" and we closed the door behind us. All of us, totally wrung out carers, walked down the corridor not saying a word until we were out of earshot, then we cracked up and laughed. Well, maybe it hadn't looked as bad as we first thought; maybe if we had been sitting in the audience we would have seen the funny side of it. We had been so ticked off with Will we hadn't heard the audiences reaction, we were just too worried. Now all we had to do was make sure that when Will went to see Matron and her guests he didn't drop everyone in it and tell them that he really was drunk. It took some time to get Will to understand what he had to do and he seemed to understand so off he went. We all sat and awaited his return. He wasn't long so we knew he hadn't let us down.

"All they wanted to do was praise me up, they wouldn't let me say anything" he said.

"Thank goodness for that" we said as we sipped on the rice wine that Eric had hidden under his bed. He decided that we could have a nip because as he said 'Yo look as though yo need summat.' Bless him.

The meeting with Matron went well she really wasn't that angry after all everything had worked out very well, but she did say as we went.

"Get rid of that feckin wine." We scurried off to the staff room where some of the other staff had heard about our fracas and wanted to know the outcome. So, once again the staff room was clouding over with smoke, with the sound of care staff laughing and swearing and all agreeing to do the same next year. I turned to Jen.

"Some hope of that," I said.

Chapter 8

Life carried on with coughs and colds, little accidents with good care and a lot of TLC, most problems were overcome easily. Before we knew it Easter was around the corner and bonnets were in the process of being made, with a certain amount of rivalry between units as to who could make the best ones and who would be wearing them. We enjoyed every moment and our residents helped where they could. We ended up making ten bonnets and even the men wanted to take part. The staff decided not to make special hats for the men, if they wanted to take part they would have to help make the bonnets themselves. That way they couldn't blame us if they looked silly. They really got into the swing of it Eric decided his hat would just be a rabbit with a ribbon tied around it and a big bow under his chin. It looked really daft and suited him so he paraded around the unit showing off. This irritated Will so of course his bonnet had to be better; he took himself off to his room with ribbons and cardboard shouting as he went.

"I'll show him who can make the best bonnet." He wouldn't let anyone near his room until the Easter Bonnet parade had begun. Everyone was eager to see his masterpiece and with all our residents up in the main hall Will sat until all the other guests had arrived.

Matron had as usual invited some residents from other homes to take part. We were all enjoying the party, then our fourth officer Jill decided it would be a good idea to hold a raffle and she nominated some of the staff to go round with a book of tickets. Unfortunately Jill didn't have very good communication skills and instead of asking some of the staff she ordered Lil off Ash unit to sell the tickets. Now

Lil didn't like this she felt like it wasn't her job and she told Jill so. Jill in turn got all uppity and once again asked Lil to go round with the tickets, whereby Lil told her where to stick them. Now we all knew this was not a very good idea, I quickly stepped forward and volunteered to do it but by now it had become a matter of principal and Jill felt her authority was being put to the test so she dug her heels in and wouldn't back down.

Matron noticed the commotion in the corridor and stepped in, she closed the connecting doors and shooed the staff out who had only been there for a bit of a nose. We could see through the glass panel as Jill (now all calm and in control) related what the problem was, with Lil staring straight back at her and not giving her one inch. Just as we were expecting Lil to march out Matron took the tickets out of Lil's hand and gave them to Jill. They turned towards the corridor where we had all merged with the other revelers but still kept a good eye on the proceedings. Out came Jill and Matron, bringing up the rear was our Lil all smiles nodding as she came in our direction. Then to our amazement Jill AND Lil started selling the tickets together. We almost fell off our feet and couldn't wait to hear what had gone on. We would have to wait for tomorrows break because the party was now ready for the Easter Bonnet Parade and someone had to go and get our Will. Carol and I raced down onto the unit and tapped on Wills door.

"Come on Will" we called "It's time." Will didn't answer so we called louder; we were getting worried so we decided to go in just in case Will had lost his nerve. There was Will with the biggest rabbit and ribbon perched on his head, now where had he got that from (we later found out) but at that moment we had lost all interest. Will was lying on his bed as though he had been on his bed for some time waiting for his big moment, but the knock he had waited for hadn't come fast enough.

Will had suffered a massive heart attack, the Doctor later said we wouldn't have been able to save him even if we had been in the room at the time (at times like this my job is really terrible and we have all at some time asked ourselves why we do it). There Will lay with his hat on, looking really sad and alone, we both raced to where Will lay and I checked his pulse, we both knew it was no use. We held his hand and started to cry.

"Oh Will, why didn't you wait for someone to be with you?"

We pulled the emergency cord and asked Matron to come to Wills room (now when someone dies you aren't allowed to touch the body in any way, you have to wait for the Doctor, the coroner comes too and sometimes the police). We sat and cried Will looked so silly with his hat on, we wanted to take it off at least then he would have some dignity. Matron came down and asked us to stay with him until she had got in touch with the Doctor and we were glad of that because we really didn't have the heart to go back to the party.

The Doctor came and the process carried on (the Co-op funeral Director came later on to take Will away). Our residents knew something was going on but we didn't have the heart to tell them, not yet anyhow. Eric knocked on Wills door and asked if his mate was OK and if he knew whether he had won the prize for best hat.

"No Eric" we said, we hadn't told him.

"Oh OK" Eric said "I don't like this type of Whisky and wondered if you could give it to Will, it may make him feel better if he could chuck it back at me" he said with a sheepish grin.

"Thanks Eric I will make sure Will gets it but I wouldn't bother ducking, Will won't be throwing anything from now on."

"Oh, God" said Eric backing away from Will's door and into his own.

Eric took Will's death really very bad, the fighting spirit went out of his life that night. Will hadn't got many relatives and his funeral was very sad, all the staff went from Beech unit. Even though Will was a handful sometimes he was a great personality and was really missed not least by Eric.

"Sometimes I really hate this job" I said and we all agreed.

Tarar Will.

Chapter 9

Two weeks had passed since Will's funeral and we had been really surprised at how the other residents had reacted. There had been no tears from them, once the funeral was over the conversation had been quite cheerful and they were looking forward to who was coming on the unit next. The routine when someone passes away if they had a single room is for the occupant of a double room (usually the one that had been there the longest) to have the choice of a single room. Because we had lost a male resident Matron thought it would be best if we had another male to take his place. So, the ladies in the double weren't asked, fortunately this didn't worry them as they enjoyed each other's company and didn't want to be moved.

Eric was the only one that had been really changed by Will's death, he always stayed in his room now. His family brought him a TV and he had no one to keep him on his toes, so there he stayed only coming out for meals and the odd cuppa. We had been worried but Matron called us together and explained that Eric needed time to grieve in his own way, so we backed off, only popping into his room to make sure he was ok.

Word got around that we were having a new resident, his name was David and he was coming straight from the hospital due to a fall he'd had. He was living on his own in a flat with his family looking after him but this fall was the last of many. The family had made the decision that it would be best for David to have 24/7 care. His family had been in sometime last week to have a look around, see where David's room was and what they could bring in for him that would make the move easier. They had already brought him a colour TV and had a phone put in so all that was needed was for David to come in with a few of his things.

We told Eric what was happening but he didn't seem to care, he didn't say a lot only.

"Just you tell him, I won't stand any daftness". He said "and make sure he keeps his telly down too I don't want to hear his telly over mine!" That's great we all thought this poor chap, new to residential care and about to make an enemy even before he had even come in.

David came with about six members of his family all popping in and out with this and that. They had made his room really comfortable with his own TV chair by the widow, bedside lamps, photos and pictures. We thought Eric would have shouted out for them to shut the noise up but he just sat there, we waited for the balloon to go up but it never did, which is a pity really it would have been good for Eric (but not for David). Still it never happened so we all heaved a sigh of relief when the family were satisfied that their dad had everything he wanted.

David walked with the aid of a Zimmer, now he had been given it in hospital and had got used to it really well; the only problem was that David still counted out loud as he walked. You could always hear him muttering then moving the frame.

"One, two" move the frame "one, two" as he walked into it. David was no trouble and he settled in really well, this was due to having such a careful family who trusted in the staff, they had involved their dad in everything that was happening to him.

Slowly Eric started to come out of his room more often, we didn't make too much of a fuss and left Eric to find his own way out of his grieving. I'm sure Will would have been quite surprised at how long it had taken Eric to get over his death.

David settled in well but we were to find out David had another little problem, he wasn't incontinent but he had the largest testicles I had ever seen. This wasn't the problem though, it was the fact that his penis was so small, which again wasn't a problem in itself, but taking him to the loo was an ordeal and a half! If he had to sit on the loo it meant that David's little penis was pushed well down under the loo seat, just that little space between the loo itself and the loo seat. Now it was getting quite normal to hear shouts of "Oh, no!" from the loo when David was in because no matter how we sat him on the toilet his little penis would find its way up a little, just enough to wee on any unsuspecting staff that happened to be in his line of fire. No matter how you pushed his bits and pieces down at the critical moment, up it would come and 'wham' another wet over-all (it's funny how you get used to being weed on and sometimes 'the other' on).

David at first would wonder what was happening and would always have a good old laugh at the staff that were dancing about trying to get out of the little stream of wee. We learned after a while how to manage David; he had to use the lower toilet which was easier for him to lean forward on and keep his willy in check.

On one occasion David really needed the toilet but the lower toilet was in use, we asked David if he could wait and he seemed OK, but minutes seemed like a long time with a bursting bladder and David was getting a little impatient. When Jill, our fourth officer came down with the post, David once again asked if he could go.

"Yes David, you can go in just a second, we'll just see to Elsie's leg dressing." I answered.

"OK" he said.

Then Jill piped up "Come on David, let me take you."

"No, no I'll wait" he said.

84

Well at this Jill took offence "David, I do know what you have to do you know, I've been doing this job for years, now come on matey, off we go." She said.

Sylv and I looked at each other "you'll find the lower seat much better" one of us said to her.

"Don't be silly" Jill called over her shoulder "this toilet is much better for David's height."

Well what could we do, we looked at David and the little devil winked at us as he carried on with his frame "One, two, one, two."

It was only moments before we heard her cry.

"Argh! Oh my God!" Jill bounded out of the loo shouting "Why the hell didn't you warn me?"

Jill started to giggle but once again I couldn't stand it and came out with one big loud laugh.

"Ha, Ha, Ha" I really couldn't help myself. Jill scurried off up the corridor muttering something like 'bloody stupid man'.

We finished Elsie's dressing on her leg and went into David, hoping to find the words to make him feel better but as we did we could hear him laughing to himself and when we got to him he laughed out loud, joining Sylv and I. We found out a lot about David that day the little devil, but what a sense of humour.

Matron called a staff meeting for everyone to attend, the agenda was the summer fete. Some of us remembered the fete at The Miles so we hoped it would be the same. The only difference was that we didn't have a 'League of Friends' and the home really needed this type of help, Matron hoped that this fete would help advertise that fact. The meeting went well with Matron opening up to any ideas of how we could use our main hall. Different ideas were put forward with me volunteering to start a keep fit class 'just for fun' I'd said. My idea took on a life of its own, so as well as the 'Summer Fete' posters my 'Keep Fit' posters went up as well. I went into a panic, I had done a 'just for fun' class at my daughters school which had gone very well but it had taken up a lot of my spare time. I had to work out routines to fill an hour and I had to volunteer someone to help me. I picked Pam from Oak unit, she seemed as keen as I was. So we picked out some music to do a routine to, it would have to be 'Ah, shut up a your face'. We worked well and our first class was to be when I was on duty, Pam was on a rest day but she didn't mind coming in. we were so nervous, not because we didn't know what we were doing but in case no one turned up.

Now Pam and I had brought new leotards and were swanning about looking and feeling just dandy, our residents wanted to come up to the hall too for a good laugh, we didn't care. The doors were opened and before we knew it the hall was full. At 50p a class we were quite pleased, so was Matron. Before we started we informed everyone that we were not experienced keep fit instructors and that it was just for fun so if there were any moves anyone couldn't manage, they could just march it through until they were ready to join in again.

When you're at the front of a group of people and the music is pumping, the adrenaline is great, just how much do you push yourself?

"OK ladies, let's go" and off we went. It was going well, I was at the front and Pam stood at the back helping anyone that needed it.

"Two, three, four, down, two, three, four, up, two three, four...Now everyone lie on the floor and slowly and gently lift your feet off the floor, OK, keep going and see how far you can stretch them over your head. Good!" I called above the music.

Well Pam started to laugh at the back, while I couldn't see what was happening she could see that some of the ladies had rolled over onto their sides and then onto their knees and crawled off in single file down the corridor. I was left with about ten ladies all grunting and groaning with their legs in the air. "OK ladies, gently roll onto your sides and stand up." By the time we stood up Pam was nowhere to be seen and we could hear the laughter coming from the staff room, the rest of us couldn't stand it much longer and we ran to find them all sitting with their feet up smoking and drinking a bottle of wine that had been brought in by someone to celebrate our first night. My ladies gave in and decided to join them. The first keep fit had gone well and everyone had really enjoyed it and promised to come back next week. They were as good as their word bringing with them other friends, the hall ended up being the talk of the area just what Matron had wanted. The keep fit carried on and was doing really well and it was earning the home about fifteen pounds a week. This doesn't seem a lot but every little helps and our home was now open to the community. I was getting really fit now and became quite a poser in my new leotard.

Our Summer Fete was to be held at the end of July, we were having a bouncy castle, tombola, smash the rat, craft stalls and baby shows, all was ready. Matron had decided to go on holiday just before the Fete but assured us that she would be back in time. We worked hard encouraging the residents to knit like mad making blankets, loo roll holders and coat hanger covers. The weather was lovely and we all looked forward to the day that Matron went on holiday. It may have been stress but Jill went power crazy, she became unbearable and the other officers tried to take no notice but really were waiting to relate all to Matron on her return.

Our keep fit class was on a Friday and I stood with Pam waiting for our ladies to arrive with the usual chatter and giggling at each other's outfits.

"Come on then you lot" I called "let's get going" Again I was really on duty but Matron always made sure our unit was covered by the staff that weren't interested in the keep fit. Jill came down and stood and watched our routine, I thought she was just showing an interest so I carried on.

"Legs in the air...one two and stretch them round your neck... three, four." This was really funny but Jill just stood and glared, I carried on wondering why she didn't just join in or clear off. We had a break half time and we were ready for it, I switched the record player off straight away and turned round and Jill was there.

"Come with me Jackie, I want to speak to you in my office." Jill said in a really firm tone.

"Oh, right" I said still not really knowing what was going on in her mind. I turned around and saw Pam looking on and wondering what the problem was. Jill didn't say anything until the office door had been closed, then she just let rip, she verbally flew at me.

"What the hell do you think you are doing?" she bellowed.

"I don't understand what you mean?" I tried to answer but she was having none of it.

"Who the hell gave you permission to do this class with Matron away?"

"Well it's a weekly thing now" I said "Matron always has my shift covered."

"Jackie you should have come to me before you organised this week's class." Just then the door knocked.

"Wait!" Called Jill as she carried on flying at me. I was by now really upset at the outburst and was wondering what to say when the office door burst open and there stood some of my ladies with Pam all ready to have a go at Jill.

"Get out." Said Jill "Just get out!"

"Oh shut up" one of my ladies said back.

"None of this is Jackie's fault, it's you lot up here in the office, lack of communication, you knew about the class and I'm sure Matron had it covered before she left" argued Pam.

"Not that it's any of your business" said Jill to Pam. She looked at me and said "your unit isn't covered and you are needed Jackie."

"Well that's no reason for you to have a go at me, if I had been told Pam could have taken over." I said finding the courage to speak up but it was all in vein and the meeting was over. Jill really did have a problem with communication and I thought just wait for Matron to come back because I for one would never do a class again, it was becoming too much for me. The other officers heard about the outburst and they were all on my side but this didn't really help how I was feeling, I felt as though it had all been my fault. Everyone had backed me up but that day had been by far my worst day on duty at the home so far. After all, I thought, I had been helping Matron with her ideas about opening the home to the public.

Matron came back from her holiday and before she was due back she came to see me, she was really bothered about what she had heard. Jill didn't realise it at the time and neither did I but Matron had friends that attended the keep fit class and they had told Matron what happened even before the officers had time to put their two-penneth in. Matron apologised and said it would never happen again. I had to say I knew it wouldn't because I wouldn't be doing another class, I was sorry and I had already organised for someone to take over next week. It would be different because the other lady wanted to take the class a bit further and be more professional.

"I don't want anyone else running the class" she almost shouted. I had to stand my ground now and I was really upset about the whole thing because I was worried about Jill really having it in for me, after all she could make my life hell and Matron wouldn't be there all the time (I'm not the sort of person to complain it just isn't my way; I'd rather deal with people straight to their faces).

Matron couldn't reverse my decision and went off up the corridor in rather a bad mood. She left the building without speaking to any one; the other officers came down to see me and were all in complete agreement. Jill just couldn't cope with the stress of being in her own office. When Matron was due to start her duties a notice went up for a staff meeting:

Agenda – Staff Morale

The meeting was attended by nearly all the staff, all the officers too, even Jill sat facing us. At this point I didn't have a problem, I didn't see much of her and that was fine with me. The meeting was very strained and it was put to everyone that I was giving up the keep fit and that Matron was very disappointed with my decision but I couldn't be persuaded to carry on. Things were a little difficult for a while after this and Jill seemed to be on other shifts to me. Matron did this for my benefit and I was really grateful for it.

Keep fit carried on for a while but the old troop stopped coming even Matrons friends and eventually it stopped altogether which was a real shame. Funnily enough the whole incident didn't stop me from volunteering for other things in the future but I always made sure I was off duty and gave the home many hours of my own time, not out of silliness but for my own piece of mind. I never wanted to be in that situation ever again (mind you it did show me who my real friends were and that was really comforting).

The sun was shining, the birds were coughing and all was right with the home.

Chapter 10

The day of the summer fete had arrived and we were all looking forward to it. There was a plan in the staff room indicating where all the stalls had to go, with our stall in prime place in the main hall. We had managed to get a good pitch because two of our residents had volunteered to run it for us with a little help from the care staff of course. The summer fete was always a good chance for the care staff to not only make money for the unit but have a good time as well so we all wanted to help. These chances didn't come round very often so if we didn't have to work some of us usually came back to make up the numbers. Beech unit with the help of the residents had decided to have a 'Bash the Rat' stall which involved a very long piece of tube that we begged from the local carpet shop in the village and a nice big rubber hammer. Eric and David had made the stall sign 'Bash a Rat – 20p a Bash!' in nice big letters. They had wanted to paint it in blood red, but the other residents didn't think this would have been in good taste, still quite imaginative we thought. Well, this stall was new it had been Lena herself that had thought of it so naturally we volunteered her into the post, she in turn had decided that if she had to help it was only fair that Miss Trent helped with all the fun as well. Lena had been practicing her 'call' ever since we had volunteered her and we had all agreed she did the job quite noisily enough. After hearing it for two or three months now we had all had enough, to the point that some of the other residents had fallen out with the pair. Freda had even called from her bedroom one night.

"Shut the bloody row!" We usually loved it when a little fracas happened, it was quite an eye opener when they could be at each other's necks one minute and best of friends the next. Miss Trent had said from the beginning that if she had been expected to call like some sort of market trader then quite obviously she couldn't help as she hadn't shouted out like that in her life and she wasn't going to start now. Lena didn't mind she was loud enough for them both she boasted.

The doors were opened and the crowds pushed in, we stood there ready to make a fortune, Miss Trent on the money box and Lena in full voice.

"Come and bash a rat me lovely, 20p a bash!" Carol and I helped the two ladies until we realised they could manage on their own for a little while, so we decided to have a little skive and enjoy a hot dog or two. The beer tent was doing a roaring trade and you could hear the football chatter flowing like waves as you walked around the stalls. Mothers were pulling children away from the bouncy castle.

"Yes you can have another go as soon as we find your father to get a bit more cash" they would say and "no, you can't have another hot dog, wait for your tea."

The weather was very hot and as the day wore on mothers and children were starting to wonder where their men and daddies had gone to and how long they would be. Still they bimbled about, children pulling on pushchairs, wandering to this stall and that pushing ice creams into little hands to quieten them while mommy tried to win a bottle of bubbly from the tombola stall. Some children had decided that it was all too boring and had ambushed the bouncy castle. A large mountain of shoes had now piled up with Sylv shouting at the children.

"Now, now children can you make a nice orderly queue and wait your turn."

This little speech was totally wasted on the little gang of bouncers but Sylv felt she had to try and get some sort of order. Carol and I looked at each other, then at the jumble of fun and felt we should do something to help, but then again it would be a shame to split this up now, it would be a good conversation piece back in the sanity of the staff room tomorrow. So we wandered off and had a cup of tea promising to take one back to our two 'Bash a Rat' stars. We found we could hear Lena above the crowd so we knew things were all OK.

After taking Lena and Miss Trent their cuppa's, Matron asked us to go round and pick up all the monies from the stalls so she could start and add up the takings. By the time we had got back to poor Sylv with the mountain of shoes all we could hear was.

"Well, I haven't had your kid's bloody shoes." Poor Sylv, now sweating with frustration and heat, was in the process of ramming any shoe onto any foot, boys or girls, big or small, while giggling children twisted and turned trying desperately to pull little feet away and get back on the bouncy castle with their new mates. Mothers were to be heard much later on calling over the tannoy for odd shoes to be returned. We decided to tip toe past and go back later for Sylv's money. The tombola stall had as usual done very well and some of the staff that had been lumbered with the craft and gift stalls were still having a moan. Gift and craft stalls never did much, they always had to cover the cost of making so normally out priced themselves, people just wanted a bargain and anything that cost over a pound was daylight robbery, or so we heard them mutter as they went off to the jumble sale stall. It was about then that we heard a far off rumble, something was going on in the hall, the beer tent was unusually quiet, a commotion was brewing and it seemed to be coming from our 'Bash a Rat' stall. When we arrived all we could hear were mothers shouting.

"Let the doll go, for goodness sake."

While the men, now a little worse from drink and heat were calling out.

"Just let the bloody doll go. I've paid for a go and I'm entitled to a bloody go."

Mothers were pulling at the hammer; children were shouting.

"No Mommy, don't let them bash the Dolly!"

Lena was trying to quite the situation down while some children had decided to take the matter into their own hands and were pulling the rubber hammer out of their mommy's hands while belting the occasional passing toddler or pet with it, causing more arguing. It was all a terrible mess and if Matron heard it we would all be in very big trouble, on-lookers were finding it all very funny and even Sylv had stopped throwing shoes about to see what was going on. By the time we had pushed our way through the crowd we could see Miss Trent holding what looked like a little raggy doll up over her head, the raggy 'rat' was under the table with the stuffing knocked out of it. Lena, we found out later, had thrown it there because of the state it was in, it wouldn't go down the tube properly and had found the raggy doll as a replacement, but Miss Trent had felt sorry for the little unloved raggy doll and wouldn't let the men bash it. Now big boys, with a little drink inside them found the whole thing a matter of principle and treated it like some sort of commando operation and wanted to take their aggression out on the poor little dolly Miss Trent had taken a shine to. All Miss Trent had to do was push the dolly down the tube and they would bash the be'jesus out of it. Carol and I pushed our way through the crowd and tried to close the stall to give the men their money back but oh no, they didn't want their money back, they liked this stall and wanted to know where they could get one from.

94

"What a con, they've had our money, now they won't let us have a go" they called and "come on giz a go." Beer merry men can be a real pain, they thought it was a real joke but poor Miss Trent couldn't bring herself to release that dolly. While I tried to talk to Miss Trent, Carol raced about trying to find a substitute. It seemed like hours before she came back and when she did she was clutching a well-worn 'Kermit'. When Miss Trent saw it she made a grab for that too but I managed to get her outside where she sat on the bench and accepted a half pint of shandy. We sat listening to sound of merry men.

"Yeah!"

"Ah ha, ya missed, ya daft bugger."

"Get ya glasses on ya old fool."

Bang as the hammer hit the table and a new call echoed out. This was all a bit too much for Miss Trent and I decided to take her up to Matron (I felt really sorry for Miss Trent that day she wasn't usually like that and had been fine while it had been a rat that was being bashed but there was something about that dolly. We found out later on what the problem had been but it was much later on). I raced back to the stall with Matrons orders to close it down once and for all. As I entered the hall I realised the commotion had encouraged many more 'beer tent chappies' to come and see what all the fun was about so I had quite a push to get back to Carol to tell her what Matron had said. The merry chaps were now pushing kiddies out of the way while others were picking them up and calling.

"Here mother, make yourself useful and hold on to him a minute, let me show this hopeless lot how to do it."

It was being treated like some sort of battle; Miss Trent needn't have worried about the new little dolly because the merry chaps missed more than they hit but continued to throw their money into the money tin, never asking for change so we didn't mind. How on earth were we going to put a stop to this, I certainly wasn't going to call a halt the men would have gone mad again. It had become a competition between two groups of men and they were tripping over each other as they moved in to have another go, arms sliding across the table, thumbs acting like gun sights as they lined up the hammer.

"Now!"

"Go on man, bash it!"

One chap shot the dolly down the tube at such a speed it shot out, skimmed the table and landed in Matrons hand.

"What a catch" someone called and a cheer went up changing the mood of the crowd. "Three cheers for Matron" some carried on "who knows how to put on a blinkin good fete. Hip hip horay."

"OK fellas," Matron smiled "how about one of you owning this attraction?" she said. Another cheer went up and the staff who had turned up to see how this would turn out watched eagerly.

"We'll have an auction." She said, all the merry men agreed, while the wives, girlfriends and children didn't. The children wondered what all the fuss was about as they bounded under the table to find any money that had bounced out of the money tin that the chaps had been throwing into willy-nilly. Little titters could be heard as they counted up their finds. Matron managed to retrieve the hammer and stood on the chair in front of her.

"Let's start," she said "who wants to take this game home with them this afternoon?" The calls went up and the bidding started at 50p with some silly chaps outbidding themselves by calling too quick. All the mothers and girlfriends at this point seemed at the same time to give a sigh, pulling the children away and heading off to the beer tent saying come on let's go and get a drink and off the crowd went leaving their men to it.

The men had reached fifteen pounds; chaps were gathered together adding up how much they had left in their pockets so they could outbid the other team. Fifteen fifty, sixteen, seventeen, Matron waited until she thought they had run out of money, mainly so they couldn't go back to their beer tent that was now in the process of cleaning up. Smiling little men with bulging purses from a good days takings were humming and tidying up with brushes and sticks with spikes on the ends of them. They flattered their way around mothers and girlfriends who were all planning how they would get their own back on the men.

"Oh well they'll want their tea when they get in," someone said.

"Well they can bloomin well think again. It's still too hot and I can't be bothered."

"If we work it right the daft lot won't know what day it is never mind if they have had any tea or not."

"Just look at them, if you put all the brains in that group together you wouldn't come up with one that worked." Someone laughed

"Yeah, that goes for the other parts as well."

"Ha, ha, mine doesn't need a drink for that to happen." Someone else piped up "anyone fancy coming back to mine for a coffee?" Off they went pulling pushchairs and kids with them and having a good laugh as they went. The men were down to their last pennies.

"You'll have the droppings from our noses wont ya Matron" one called "come on bang that bloody hammer."

"OK, if all the biddings done?"

"Oh come on" someone shouted, I need a pee."

"At the grand total of twenty pounds and fifty pence" Matron pointed "the 'Bash a Rat' goes to Sam, the man over there in the flat cap." A cheer went up and the tube, hammer and little dolly left the hall, zigzagging up the road with a file of wandering men following singing "Hello Dolly" to the poor little doll as they went.

Back at the home the counting was still going on, we felt sure we had actually made more than the tombola stall this year and that hadn't happened before or at least not for as long as we could remember.

Once everything had been put away and our residents were relaxing with their supper drinks Matron came down to the staff room and announced the total.

"Six hundred pounds and twenty five pence!" We were breathless and Matron was over the moon. "We should now have enough for a new large screen TV and video player for the hall." Matron had wanted this for ages it was an idea she had back at The Miles and it meant we could now have our own film show nights with our residents clubbing together to rent their favourite films. Our stall with all its ups and downs had totalled fifty pounds and two pence and had beaten the tombola by one pound, not a lot but we had it.

"Yeah" a little cheer went up from Carol and I, it had been a hard busy day, but a good one.

The local newspapers had been good to us Matron said the next day at report, they had left before the fracas had happened. Matron congratulated us all again on the fete's success then carried on.

"While I have you all here and in good spirit we can start thinking about the Christmas concert or pantomime so thinking hats on, we'll be having a meeting soon to discuss any ideas OK" she said "all your residents have had good nights with no problems so off you go and keep it that way." We all streamed out of the office still with yesterday very much on our minds.

"Yeah we saw you having trouble" we said to Sylv "but you looked as though you were coping so we left you to it."

"Oh thanks a lot you rotten swines, I still have two pairs of lost shoes to find, goodness knows where they went!" she called as she went up the corridor to her own unit.

Chapter 11

I can't remember when Elsie's problem first showed itself. Elsie looked after Kate so well we were confident that if she was having any trouble or it was becoming too much, she would let us know, so sometimes we seemed to overlook our Elsie. She was such a bustling little lady with a great deal of personality, she really didn't like us taking over (as she had said once when she hadn't long moved in). So we coped with the other eight residents and Elsie coped with Kate, and we in our ignorance failed to see that Elsie was having trouble.

Kate saw Elsie as a spring chicken and expected everything done for her and at speed too, eventually we noticed how it was taking Elsie longer to get Kate up in the mornings. We had left it for a little while hoping Elsie would come to us if there was a problem. We didn't want Elsie thinking we were criticizing her ability to care for her sister; this would really upset her in all sorts of ways, after all Elsie took great pride in how well she looked after her sister. She also made sure everyone knew about it, enjoying all the praise that came her way. You could hear her as she cleaned their room singing some of the old songs with Kate joining in on the odd occasion. The singing cheered the unit up on many a rainy day, but on this particular morning Elsie had brought Kate out for her breakfast much later than usual so as I popped my head round the bedroom door I called.

"You OK Elsie, do you need a hand there?"

There was Elsie proceeding to pull the bedside cabinet away from the wall.

"What are you doing?" I asked as I helped pull the cabinet. Elsie had a bowl of water with detergent in it and a large white cleaning rag in her hand.

"Are you coming for your breakfast before you start cleaning Elsie?" I asked "Surely you need a good cuppa to start the day."

"No, I'm fine" Elsie said from behind the cabinet "just bring it in here and I'll drink it as I go. Don't start worrying your head about me girl." She called over her shoulder as she continued to clean the sides of the cabinet, but I was worried, I hadn't noticed this behaviour before. I decided to go and ask Kate how long this had been going on.

"Oh well" Kate replied, "Elsie has to do her cleaning, I told her not to bother so much but she wouldn't listen to me. Now she feels she's all behind with her work, you know how it is with her." Then Kate proceeded to eat her breakfast while she listed all her ailments.

When Elsie didn't come out for her breakfast I left Kate and went back to Elsie to see where she was. She was still standing by the cabinet which had been cleaned and polished and I could smell polish mixed with the smell of soap. Elsie was looking at the cabinet with her head on one side.

"Is that where it came from Jackie?" she asked pointing at the carpet.

"Well" I answered. I think so by the imprint on the carpet, you have it in exactly the same place.

"Oh right" she said but still proceeded to shove it this way and that until I felt myself getting a little annoyed with the silly situation.

"Now come on our Elsie" I said "I think you have it about right, shall we go and see how our Kate is in the other room?" To my amazement she just turned and went to the sink.

"I'll just wash my hands" she said "They do smell of polish."

101

"OK" I said and I left her to it. I thought it would be a good idea to let Carol know what I had been doing all this time and see if she had noticed any funny behaviour from Elsie. She had been as surprised as I had been and what we hadn't bargained for was Elsie being Ill before Kate. Still hindsight is a wonderful thing, we read all the reports from a couple of weeks ago but nothing had been reported from other staff. We decided we would have a chat with Elsie then go and see Matron. Back in Elsie's room she was still washing her hands, drying them then washing them again.

"What are you doing our Elsie?" we asked.

"Well I think I need a clean towel, every time I dry my hands I need to wash them again because of the towel" she said this really to herself "I'll just leave them to dry themselves that's the best isn't it?" and she now looked at us for reassurance.

"Oh yes that's fine Elsie, make sure you have a few towels in your room just in case. How's that, will that do?"

Elsie looked at me with tears in her eyes.

"Thanks Jackie, I knew you would understand."

Well I had heard of compulsive disorders before but had never come into contact with it and we really didn't know enough about it. To be of any help what we both knew was that Elsie needed more help as this behaviour was wearing her out. Thank goodness we had found the problem and it could be dealt with.

When Elsie was happy to leave her room and go with Carol to sit with Kate I had a good chance to have a look around Elsie's room, there was no denying it she kept the room beautiful, it smelt of soap, lovely and clean smelling. Then I noticed the doors on the wardrobe were losing their varnish and the chest of drawers were the same, they were starting to look a bit dull. Elsie had been washing the bedroom furniture with soap before polishing it, as I sat on the edge of the bed I wondered just how long this had been going on and just what time in the morning she started her cleaning. The night staff would have only popped in if there had been a problem reported, so as long as they just heard them talking in the morning they wouldn't have known there was a problem. I decided to have a peep into the wardrobe to see if the inside was the same but that looked OK, what I did notice though was a large shopping bag and when I looked inside it was full of soap, all the same brand and all opened. The smell was almost too much, I sat back on the bed and felt so sorry for poor Elsie and really annoyed at myself for not noticing there was a problem. Matron would have to be told.

Elsie's daughter had been informed and she was very pleased we had picked it up so quickly. We were all amazed to hear that apparently Elsie had suffered with the same thing years ago. A unit meeting was called for the following week to see what we could do to help; we decided to tread very carefully. Matron also came down to speak to all of the residents and she explained that all cleaning cupboards had to be kept locked, she was sorry about it but these new rules had come from the top and if anyone wanted to complain she had the number in her office and to be her guest. We all hoped this tactic would stop Elsie from using so much polish etc. This didn't stop our Elsie, all she did was substitute the polish and disinfectant with hand soap, the same procedure carried on each morning with breakfast being delayed. Soap started vanishing at an alarming rate from all over the home yet no one saw Elsie actually help herself from the bathrooms and toilets.

Pocket money day was becoming a nightmare because Elsie felt she had to have Kate's money as well but Kate wanted it herself even though she never did anything with it except give it to her daughter when she visited. Unfortunately Elsie started to get very agitated on Thursday's, from early in the morning she kept a sharp look out for Matron coming down with the pocket money, she would sit in the corridor and hijack her, making sure she had it before Kate. Elsie said it had to be washed and dried properly getting rid of any germs that might be on it before Kate could have it. Now for us carers this was getting to be a proper pain in the neck, Elsie was really lovely but this just wasn't funny and we could see how much the whole thing was wearing her out. She wasn't eating properly any more, her appearance was suffering and she looked tired all the time. The Doctor had been called but all he would say was to prescribe anti-depressants which made Elsie unsteady on her feet.

It was while she was on these tablets that she had a fall, it was in the middle of the night while she was on one of her soap raids (we found out she would go round the home while everyone was asleep and collect all the soaps, putting them into her carrier bag), unfortunately on one occasion she had dropped a tablet of soap and while looking for it had trodden on it. Consequently she had a nasty fall, breaking her wrist in the process!

Poor old Elsie never really got over that fall and because she had great difficulty washing now, mentally she just went from bad to worse. The funny thing was Kate didn't really worry about her sister it all seemed quite normal for her as she had said to her time and time again.

"You will kill yourself with all that washing."

Oddly enough that is really what happened in a roundabout sort of way.

Chapter 12

Matron often had to go to 'heads of homes' meetings and most of the time she enjoyed them but on one particular occasion she had been told of a new working practice that had to be tried out. It involved moving staff around the units with a six week rotation. We were not amused and neither was Matron but our residents were really looking forward to it.

"Thanks a lot" we said as we picked up our bits and pieces and moaned all the way up the corridor with a ciggie stop on the way. Our residents were looking forward to it mainly because they knew what they could and couldn't get away with if we weren't around. If a new or different staff member came onto the unit you could bet at least one resident would put themselves into a wheelchair. The problem with that was, once in there it was virtually impossible to get them walking again, not because they couldn't but because they preferred not to walk when they could ride. Unfortunately along with putting themselves into a wheelchair it also meant within a short length of time, transferring became a problem. Then the resident would start to become more dependent on the staff to do some of the more basic things, this was no problem to the staff but you often saw a decline in independence and pride went with it. Before twelve months was up an independent, motivated, well dressed resident became totally dependent, frustrated and angry. So we all had to work together to keep our residents well motivated and mentally stimulated even when they (who we came to care for greatly) would have preferred to give up.

We were to go onto Ash unit for our first six weeks and Jen and I were beginning to look forward to it as all it meant was getting to know ten residents all over again while looking out for the ones that would try and pull the wool over our eyes. We had read the IPP's (individual personal profiles) but that was only the medical side of things; who had what, when, where and how. The 'person' side of things we could only find out from the staff that had been looking after them and then you had to remember it all. We found the whole thing really hard and Matron wasn't happy with staff popping up and down with all sorts of questions. Some of the staff were also questioning how another team had approached a particular problem with a resident when they did things differently on their own unit. It was hell and the residents loved it, all of a sudden we could see little groups of residents getting together, we were sure they were organising a little campaign of sabotage. The first few days passed without our residents being too upset by the upheaval and change of staff. Bath nights though had been a bit of a learning experience as Ash unit didn't have a proper bath it had a Medi-bath. The staff off Beech hadn't needed to use it, we had practiced before the home opened but that was about all. So when we came to use it, it had been quite and ordeal as we had to show the residents we were confident even though we weren't at all!

On one particular night duty I was working with Jen and it was Kay's bath night. Now Kay liked a laugh she also loved her baths and she would sit for half an hour just enjoying the warm water, she liked the water as high as it would go. Now, a Medi-bath is shaped like a very large box with a shower attachment over the top, the front of the Medi was a water tight door that locked and the bath plug was a large heavy ball on a chain that just wedged over the plug hole, no problem it was easy to use if you had a resident (like Kay) who liked having a Medi-bath. So once the water was in she just sat there and soaked it was really comfortable. I let Jen get on with it while I went off for my break.

All the staff liked their break time and Matron knew the importance of them, you learn more in a good break than in any lecture, problems were solved, ideas put forward, residents discussed, marital and sexual relationships exposed, everything was discussed in that half hour (that usually stretched into three quarters). So while we were discussing some queries from one of the older members of staff as to 'what actually went on at a ladies adult party' and 'just where did that long thing with a tassel, go?' all hell broke loose!

"Aaaargh!"

We all dropped whatever it was we were holding and ran in the direction of the shout. It was Jen and she was standing in the middle of the corridor looking at the floor, arms out to her sides looking totally resigned to what had happened. When she heard us racing towards her she looked up and pointed to the bathroom, where we could now hear Kay laughing so much she could hardly get her breath. Poor Jen couldn't say a word as though she was in shock, she began to rub her leg and we noticed now a lovely big bruise just beginning to make itself known. As we got closer we noticed how the carpet in the corridor was slowly changing from light green to dark green, then as if by magic we all realised what had happened.

"Bloody hell Jen, what have you done?" Sue called.

"What does it look like you twit." Jen answered back, not too pleased.

Meanwhile Kay was still sitting in the tub laughing.

"You should have seen it Jackie" she called "blimey I've never seen so much water, it was like a tidal wave," she laughed and carried on "the door just flew open and pushed Jen over, then the water just washed out of the bathroom door and into the corridor!" While Kay was telling us this she was sat there totally in the nip! She really didn't care when other more mobile residents came to see what all the commotion was about. Everyone was chatting and laughing and Kay stood up and called for a towel, no one seemed to take any notice of her as her rather large boobs bobbed about getting chilly. We were too busy skiing about in the water getting other residents back into the lounge while tittering to each other. There was a right commotion going on and we all stopped what we were doing when we heard the words.

"What the fecking hell is going on here?" It was Matron and once again she was scratching her head wondering why she had taken on such twits as carers for this lovely home.

The weeks carried in on much the same way as it had started with some carers moaning about how clean and tidy things were now and how they weren't going to set standards when they were going to be sent off that unit again anyway. So, little jobs were being left, morale was beginning to slip and Matron wasn't pleased at the level of absenteeism. So after just a few weeks of the new change Matron decided to change us all back and 'sod the consequences!' she'd said. So the next day we all went back to our own units and we were all glad to be there.

Eric in our absence had decided to put himself in a wheelchair and his false leg had been pushed under the bed.

"Hiya" I said to Eric as he sidled back into his room mumbling as he went. He knew I had caught him out.

"We'll talk about the wheelchair later."

"Yeah, yeah" he moaned knowing it was the end of his tricks.

Later at the breakfast table Eric sat with his stick leaning against the back of his chair and David with huge grin across his face whispered.

"That's got him Jackie."

"Yeah" I answered and patted Eric's arm on the way to get the cereal.

"Oh, y'know" Eric said "It's quite nice to be on my foot again, I didn't realise how I'd missed it. I'd have gone back to it eventually y'know."

"Yeah, yeah" David said nudging Eric's arm "but by that time it would have been too late now wouldn't it?"

Anyhow we had got other things to think about. Phyl off Oak unit was getting married and we had to find ways of making her leaving day as memorable as possible with a good send off. We had two weeks to organise and collect everything. Vibrators could be heard whirring in the staff room along with bursts of laughter.

"Blooming eck, that's a big un."

"I didn't know you could get coloured ones"

"Why do they have to have different flavours?" an older member of staff asked who was looking through the condoms.

The hen night had already been set and we were all really looking forward to it. Matron had said we could use one of the bedsits for the party as long as we looked after it, so the girls that were on duty could join us after their shift without worrying about transport or getting changed. Every so often you would hear staff giggling as they waved very large knickers about, packets of condoms, rubber gloves all sorts of different red and black underwear ready to dress poor Phyl up in. She knew something was going on and we had sworn the residents to secrecy, some of them had asked their relatives to buy confetti and rice so they felt they were doing their bit to help. Poor

Phyl was suspicious but didn't dare ask, ignorance is bliss and she was a good sport knowing we wouldn't do anything too bad.

We had been in touch with Phyl's mom and arranged for her to bring a change of clothes and a camera, we all agreed the moment had to be captured and saved, but first we had the hen party. We had decided that before the hen party began properly we would let the residents give Phyl her pressie. Eric thought it should be him because he had taken a shine to Phyl and it had nearly broke his heart when he knew she was getting married. We agreed it would be a nice touch before the booze started to flow and we all got a little 'couldn't care less'ish'. A bottle of wine was given by some of the relatives that had found out about the party and had invited themselves. A little speech was given by Eric and as he gave Phyl her pressie he held onto her hand and whispered in her ear.

"I'd just like to say good luck to ya and if that chap knocks y'about you just point him in my direction an' I'll belt him with me stick."

"Oh thanks Eric" Phyl said "I'll remember that."

Once the residents had gone back to their loungers we all made our way over to the bedsit where a good spread had been put on as a pressie from Matron, the relatives followed on and the party started. The bedsit was packed to busting and the music was very sixties which suited most of the guests. It was only when 'Freddie and the Dreamers' came on that we realised how we had neglected our Phyl and how much drink she'd had. Up she went onto the bed, skirt tucked into her knickers, doing air guitar to the unforgettable 'Who wears short shorts'. For some reason unknown to us most of the relatives that had been chatting quietly (probably about the staff) decided to leave us to it and they sidled off to our great relief (we got on great with our 'rellies' but it's best not to let them see our daft side as professionalism doesn't really go with singing at the top of your voice "Who wears short shorts!").

So we all carried on, clapping to whoever took centre stage on the bed and gave a rendition of any song, made up or not according to how may drinkies they'd had. It would be about eleven pm when Matron decided we'd had enough and came over to wish Phyl good luck giving the biggest hint to pack up and for everyone to go home. We took the hint and decided we would clean the bedsit in the morning. Still laughing at the most stupid of things we made for the door with Phyl and I fourth in the conga line. When we got to the door we looked at each other, took a deep breath and both fell down on our knees, it felt like slow motion but once there we couldn't get up again, so laughing hysterically and with some of the more 'sober' mates trying to stand us up we began to pull some of the others onto their knees too.

"It's great down here!" we called, so the conga line carried on with everyone on knees, up the grassy bank to the sound of "Get off my shoe, argh!" then bump, bang, crash as we all ended up in one big pile, laughing and rolling around on the grass. We did eventually get home and we managed to get into work the next day. We had promised Matron we would clean the bed sit up and we kept our promise but it took longer than we expected, consequently Matron never let us use it again.

The day had arrived and Phyl (poor soul) hadn't a clue, we had phoned her mom and everything was in readiness, so at dinner time and with all the residents fed and watered all the staff that could come down onto beech unit had come down and had squashed into the sluice. Now there were some 'big' girls and the sluice was quite small so there was a lot of tittering and giggling with the occasional "Hey, watch my boobs." And "Blimey, I can't breathe in ere." I was waiting for Phyl to come to my aid (as I had asked to come to help with a resident) and as we heard her foot step in corridor all went quiet.

"Coo'ee!" she called and all of a sudden we we're upon her and she was carried into the bathroom, being stripped of her uniform and into her new finery of suspenders, stockings, very big and baggy knickers and matching thermal vest. Her hat was made up of rubber blown up gloves and condoms (multi coloured of course) shaving foam was added too with a good dusting of confetti.

We thought she looked great so once happy with our creation we marched her (protesting all the way) to the nearest tree that was very close to a main road. Above her head was a sign reading 'Pap your horn if you're getting married!' and of course busses and Lorries never let us down on these occasions. Phyl's mom had arrived and she was flashing away taking photos and laughing then once Phyl had been tied to the tree and couldn't escape we all belted back into the home laughing and calling back to her.

"We'll be back at home time to let you off!" We made for the small toilet window and peered out trying not to laugh at her embarrassment but still enjoying the moment.

We did eventually let Phyl off pushing her out of the door to find her way home without letting her change. She made her way home holding onto her mom's arm, both of them laughing with tears running down their faces calling back to us lot.

"Thanks girls, see you at the wedding!"

"Yeah" we called back "see ya!"

Chapter 13

Beech unit was to have another resident to replace our Elsie, Kate had been told and a respectable time had passed. Kate seemed to be looking forward to someone sharing her room again, she didn't like being on her own. Elaine's family had visited and was happy with 'our family', she had stayed for a day getting to know everyone. Kate and Elaine got on very well, we all knew it was early days but the friendship carried on well.

Elaine was from a very well to do family and they were scattered all around the country so she didn't have a lot of visitors. She had been with us just a few weeks when someone noticed that just before nine o'clock each week day evening she would take herself off to her room, get dressed up with her makeup done and hair combed and come to sit directly in front of the TV! She would wait for the news (and a particular news reader) to come on and for that half an hour Elaine would think that newsreader was talking directly to her. At first we thought it a little silly but as the days went on we realised that Elaine had a problem and it wasn't just that she had the hots for the news reader, it was that she had a problem with drink and had managed (so far) to keep it quiet from everyone. The social workers were aware but as far as they knew she hadn't had a problem for years and her drinking was under control.

Little did they know that seeing all her family when she moved in (and knowing she wouldn't see them very often) had upset her more than anyone realised and she had been popping out to get the odd bottle of sherry. There was nothing we could do but advise her of the risk she was taking of which she already knew and told us so! If Elaine wanted to drink herself to death then there was nothing we could do about it, we had been taught that the residents had the same rights as anyone and this was her home. We did monitor the drinking and tried to ration it out with her consent but most of the time she couldn't keep to it and we had to give in. We kept in touch with her family telling them the situation but in this case the family ties weren't very strong and one family member would push it onto the other with no one taking ultimate responsibility in end. Elaine knew this so the circle went on. She started cornering other relatives and pretending they were her family getting upset if they scurried off with their own mom or dad into the privacy of bedrooms or the library, something had to be done.

One day we found out she had responded to an advert in the local paper reading 'gentleman looking for suitable single lady as a companion'. We only found out when a 'gentleman' came to visit her and she was all dressed up ready to see him, she looked really lovely and was obviously excited about the meeting. Then she showed us the torn out advert.

"Oh Blimey" I said as I read it, Matron had to be told and I wasn't doing it.

John was his name and he really looked like a nice gentleman but we thought it was funny that he was happy to see someone living in a residential home, he had his own house and he still drove a car. Elaine was still a good looking lady and came from well-off folk so she seemed to fit exactly what he wanted. He visited a few times and Elaine's drinking stopped, we tried to get to know him a little better and her family were also informed (as we thought there opinion was 'if their mother wanted a man friend who were they to say otherwise). Everything settled down to a more peaceful way of life, Elaine enjoying Johns company, the other residents enjoying the fact that they now had a good subject to chat about (because Elaine was so outgoing she would tell all, even when she really should have kept certain things private). We were quite worried about her but life carried on, Eric continued to keep himself to himself (still changed by Will's death but no one could change that now), even Elaine's antics hadn't caused a smile and all he'd do as they passed holding hands was mutter under his breath.

"Bloody daft old sods, act your age." Even that was said with none of the old vigour.

Eric still managed to do most things for himself but bathing was becoming more of a problem, up until now all Eric would do was ask us to run the bathwater and he could manage the rest himself, but now we did everything. Instead of coming out to have his supper after his bath we were taking his supper into his bedroom. Eric's fluid intake had increased to the point where we thought a Doctor's appointment was necessary, test were carried out and while we waited for the results Eric started to refuse his baths. Now this wasn't like our Eric at all, he was really a very particular chap when it came to cleanliness, he never missed his shave in the mornings always adding the cologne to his rinse water and this not only made him smell very fresh but also added a masculine aroma to the corridor. Even this was starting to be missed; we had to make a joke about it, stroking his chin in the mornings and whispering.

"Come on mate, where's that lovely soft cheek then?" He usually popped back into his bedroom after breakfast but if we didn't say anything he didn't make the effort. We were all wishing the test results would come through quicker, we knew the problem was his sugar but we needed the results to give the correct medication. It had been a couple of days and Eric had taken to his bed.

"Feeling proper poorly" he had said but he was still a proud man and refused any help that wasn't needed. One evening I was helping him back into his bed and out of routine I bent to take his sock off when he shouted.

"No, don't take my sock off, leave it on." But it was too late and I had pulled it off. To my horror I then realised why Eric had been feeling so ill, his little toe was black and the colour was moving up his foot and across to the other toes. I was more taken aback and upset that Eric had felt he couldn't confide in any of us after all this time. I sat back on my heels and with my hands in my lap just looked at him.

"Oh Eric, why didn't you say anything?"

"Yeah gel and what could you have done aye?" We both knew what it was and the probable outcome.

It wasn't long after that Eric was taken into hospital; he did come home to us because not only was it our policy but because this was his home (this was the residents home and if the end had to come it came to them with people around them that had become their family and in some cases we were all they had).

The end did come, I wasn't on duty but Eric died with staff around him that really cared and had sat with him after their shift had ended just so he wouldn't be alone.

Night, night Eric. See ya.

~

Winter had come with a vengeance that year and it had started late November with very hard frosts. The driveway down to the main doors was like a skating rink and had caught out many a chattering care assistant, sending them heading for the main doors at frightening speeds usually in a very un-lady like fashion. Some of our gentleman residents had started to get up for a morning ciggy and entertainment usually having a good laugh at our expense but always with a shout of.

"You alright gel?" then a titter would escape with a puff from the ciggy catching them in the throat and making them cough.

"Bloody swines" The carers would say into their chests as they shook or dusted the snow from their clothes (one of the jobs we would do in the winter morning after the report from. Matron was to throw salt grit down the drive, saving any other professional from going arse over tip).

Another Christmas and another Christmas party had been organised but with a proper band this year with proper instruments. The party was to be held the day before Christmas Eve that suited us all. We had the usual job of putting up the decorations throughout the home and to say our ceilings were high was an understatement. The main hall and reception didn't have flat low ceilings; they followed the shape of the roof so we had to hang decorations from the rafters. Consequently we had very high and very rickety ladders and we would chose straws to see which poor sod had to go up them. Residents at our home were usually ready for a good old laugh and usually they could see a situation before we could. So when we saw the usual male crew gathering with ciggies in hand making themselves comfortable on chairs which they'd scraped along the corridors, we became a little more worried.

The day of the party arrived without any real problem, Matron had, as usual invited resident from other homes to come along mainly because our residents numbers had depleted due to families taking them out for the Christmas holidays. We were really looking forward to it but it had started to snow in the afternoon and we all thought it would only be a little flurry. It carried on snowing, the band had arrived early and had set up their gear but by now we'd had most of our invitations cancelled by phone and Matron was becoming quite worried.

"Open the bar," she had ordered. Now we didn't think this was a good idea mainly because the band was becoming a little bored as they wanted to start playing. They had already gone through their warm up session and it was still snowing. We at this point wanted Matron to send the band away, but no we had to carry on after all it was Christmas and we did have to entertain the residents.

"Spread yourselves out" Matron said hoping that by doing this it would look as though there were more of us (as everyone knows this trick does not work and all it does is just make everyone feel more embarrassed). Well it snowed and the band got through most of the contents of the bar. The residents refused to move away from their warm lounges and we couldn't blame them. We could hear the wind outside gathering up speed and causing drifts as we carried on watching the band get more and more in the party mood (all on their own). Then Matron finally made the decision to give in and let the band go, she waked over to our little group of smoking bored carers and whispered.

"Will one of you tell the band to go home" and then she was gone. We in a cloud of smoke coughed at the same time.

"Hang on, did she say one of us had to tell the now thoroughly pie-eyed band they're not needed?"

"Oh yeah" I said as I stubbed my ciggie out "and what will they say to that?" We all looked in their direction and they in ours and then they got up and started walking towards us.

"Blood hell" we said in unison.

"Come on chuck" one of them said "Let us go will ya, just listen to that bloody weather, we don't want to be stuck here all night."

We all sighed with relief.

"OK" I said with authority "do you want a hand to put your stuff away?"

So, with drums, guitars and mic's all stuffed into a rickety old van we waved them off and scurried back into the home with the winds now causing us to worry. Snow drifts were up to the windows in places and some staff had a fair way to go to get home (not me of course – sometimes living close to where you work isn't a bonus). Matron gave some of the staff permission to go home as soon as the residents had been made comfortable so with only skeleton staff we waited for the night staff to appear. We were watching out the windows as all the cars that were daft enough to be out skidded about in the drifting snow. It all looked quite lovely until we heard a terrible bang, crash! A bus had skidded into a tree on our grounds and a couple of people who were waiting to get off had been tossed into the snow (this was when busses had open back doors). Matron gave instruction for us to open the back doors and let whoever wanted, to come in and wait for the police. Most of the occupants got off and headed away but ten or twelve wandered up to our doors carrying with them the snow and throwing snowballs at anyone that was daft enough to look interested.

My husband phoned to say he couldn't get the car out and for me to start walking, he said he could meet me but he really was worried about leaving the children too long as they were in bed and he didn't want to get them up and out in this weather (even though they would have loved it). I told him I had agreed to stay here (along with some other staff) and because the night staff had phoned to say they couldn't get to work Matron was really relieved. She even suggested we carry on with the party with the people from the bus accident, the police (when they eventually arrived) and the odd resident who happened to be still awake and wandering around the home. That year the party was memorable and I do remember making a snowman at two am.

Morning came and the weather had gone from bad to worse, snow had started to melt in the night, then it had frozen now it was snowing again, the very worst combination. We had managed to get some sleep but we had all hoped we could get home today after all it was Christmas Eve! We had phoned our families and explained that the day staff were still unable to get in so we would have to struggle on as best we could. Relatives that had taken residents home phoned to say they would be keeping them a while longer because of the weather (some families were really angry that they'd had their Christmas disrupted – as though we had something to do with it).

We found we were now doing jobs we didn't usually do, bed linen had to be washed and dried ready for any accidents in the night, kitchen staff would be late so we had to do breakfast, this caused a laugh but Matron made sure we all had a good breakfast as soon as our residents had been fed. Matron had a phone call later on in the morning from the police saying the warden from across the road had been in an accident and couldn't attend the flats opposite and would she sent a couple of staff across just to check on them. Straight away Sylv and I were volunteered by Matron being the most experienced and senior staff members. Matron knew the residents across the road.

"They are a lovely bunch and quite mentally alert, so watch your step" she called to the back of our well covered heads "and don't be too long."

"What did she mean by that?" we said in unison, holding our coats close to us and being extra careful we didn't fall over on the icy roads. So sliding up the path we knocked on the first door.

"Yeah, yeah what do you want?" Came the reply.

"We've come to make sure you're OK" we called.

"Course I'm bloody OK" came the answer "now bugger off." Well I looked at Sylv and she looked at me.

"Thank you, you miserable sod." We giggled into our 'grabbed up to the chin' coats. Sylv knocked the next door, it was opened and we were inside as fast as that.

"Come in, come in. Ooh what a sodding Christmas" came the call from the kitchen "take off your coats and sit a while" she said. We sighed with relief that she was ok but couldn't really stay.

"No, sorry we can't stay" we called up the corridor to the kitchen "we have to check on the other flats and we've only been to two so far."

"OK then I won't hinder you" came the reply "but do have a seasonal sherry with me won't you, please don't refuse." Now I don't drink sherry mainly because I don't like it also it goes straight to my face making me shine like a Belisha Beacon, but I couldn't refuse, especially when a fresh looking lady with a wraparound pinny came in holding a tray with all the seasonal edibles on it.

"Now come on, sit a little, my family can't come and see me until the weather turns so you have to be my Christmas." She said. Sylv had already sat and was half way down her sherry.

"Cheers" she said as we chinked our glasses.

"Cheers" she replied in a cunning sort of way, but we took no notice and had yet another mince pie.

"Now we really do have to go" I said "we've stayed too long."

"Well that's fine" she said "now don't be strangers and a Merry Christmas to you and your families."

"Yes" we said "and to you and yours."

Once outside we realised just how strong the sherry was.

"Blimey" Sylv said "I don't mind this job at all, come on I have just seen that curtain move let's go there next" I just followed on glowing.

Once again the door was opened and this time a lovely old couple asked us in, the same ritual went on and after three sherry's and only three out of ten residents visited we both decided to refuse to go into the next flat, but when the curtains fluttered and the door opened even before we got to it we were both taken off guard. Once again we found ourselves inside and sitting with yet another sherry and chocolate biscuit in hand.

"Ok yes and thank you and Merry Christmas to you" we called as we almost fell out of the door, not holding onto our coats anymore and melting the snow on the paths, roads and gardens with the glow from our faces, tittering as we went.

"What's going on" I asked "we have six flats left to go and I don't think I'm going to make it."

"Yeah, I know the feeling" Sylv giggled "great isn't it?"

"Yeah" I replied, after the past couple of days and missing my family, I really needed this (or so I was convincing myself with every sherry). We had a couple more 'Bugger offs' but by the time we had checked on all the flats we had had enough and were beginning to get worried about going back to work.

"I am sure there are rules to cover this" I muttered feeling all of a sudden totally in charge "come on Sylv" follow me". I said as I turned towards the home. All of a sudden I saw a row of net curtains drop as though the residents inside had been watching us. I looked at Sylv and it all became very clear.

"Those bloody swines have set us up." I said to Sylv as she tried desperately to pull one glove over the other leaving one hand gloveless.

"No!" she replied looking all over the place trying to find her other glove.

"Yeah, we've been their entertainment!" I replied. We decided we would have to sneak back into the home through one of the kitchen windows and hope we could sober up before Matron saw us. Every window was closed and locked and there was no one to be found that would let us in. It was then that I remembered I had left a toilet window open on Beech and we could get in there. So off we sneaked with the occasional trip and 'Oh bum' coming from Sylv and the loud laughter that seems to happen when you've had a little too much to drink. Holding onto each other shushing and giggling we went, thinking all the time we were being quiet, we came to the toilet window.

"Go on" I said "up you go."

I gave Sylv a little push and all I heard was "Good God Jackie, I think I've broken something!"

"Shh" I called back "give me your hand and just pull me in." Well, she did! And I landed by Slyv who was still in a superman position next to the toilet where she had landed. Well, we both fell about laughing and quite certain that we had managed to get into the home unheard and undetected. Sylv was rubbing her elbow and pointing to it half laughing.

"It's broken you know, it's broken!"

"Well if it's broken you'll have to go home won't you!" Matron bellowed as the toilet door burst open. We sat on the floor in shock.

"And Jackie you can go with her." She said.

"Yes Matron" we echoed, Matron backed away from our view.

"What have you been doing?" Jen asked as she helped us up.

"We had to go and check on the flats opposite" I answered.

"That was over an hour ago" she carried on "and Matron had a phone call a few moments ago from one of the residents in the flats telling her what had happened and apparently they were all very sorry."

"Oh right" we said and looked at each other "sorry for what, they set us up!"

By the time we had managed to walk home we had started to sober up and our husbands hadn't a clue what had been going on.

Old people get bored and do some really rotten things sometimes!

~

Carol and I had been told in the morning report that we would be having a new gentleman coming in today, Wilf, he would be having Eric's old room. He had a really caring family and jointly they had decided it was time for him to come to us as he had refused to live with any of his family. This was just the sort of situation we encouraged, it was always best when the residents made the decision to move in with us themselves, that way they settled in quickly. To make things better Lena had decided to take Wilf under her wing and tell him all the ins and outs of the unit.

Wilf had a strict routine when going to bed he would take his clothes off and place them neatly folded and in the correct order. When he got up his clothes were then ready to put on, pants first, last things being his cardigan and handkerchief. Wilf had had an accident a few years ago and it had left him with a false eye. He managed well with it and settled in quickly, learning the routines of the home and making the most of it. On one occasion when Wilf hadn't been with us very long I was about to go off duty when the piper alarm went off (this was the call system residents used when they got into difficulty or couldn't do something themselves). I was the nearest and went to see what the problem was, as I got nearer to Wilfs bedroom I could hear him. He was shouting at Lena who was beginning to get very upset.

"What's the matter" she was saying "can I help?"

Wilf was getting more and more angry, he was sitting in bed clutching in temper at the rest of the bed clothes and shouting what sounded like.

"Mimieye! Mimieye!" but as I went to walk even closer to him he called even louder "Mimieye for goodness sake mimieye!"

"Ok" I called "Ok now calm down and let's start again" because I had stopped where I was he had calmed down. "Now then Wilf what's the matter?" I asked again.

"It's mimieye!" he said now breathless and pointing at the floor.

"Oh" I answered "there's something on the floor" I said not quite hearing him.

"Yeah," he shouted, "its mimieye!"

"Oh" I said and down I went on my hands and knees (and not in a very lady like way at all) with Lena wondering what I was doing. Then I found what I he had been looking for and 'it' was looking back at me.

"It's here" I said "it's your eye, it's rolled under the bed and it's fine Wilf." Oh dear, Lena then realised what was being said and why, she smiled at Wilf said goodnight and left the room. Wilf took his eye popped it into his top pyjama pocket and lay back down.

"I thought the daft old twit was going to tread on it" he said to me.

"Oh Wilf" I answered "Lena was only trying to help."

"I know that Jackie but sometimes I can't find the patience to be tactful, I'll talk to her tomorrow." He said.

"OK Wilf" I replied. I walked up the corridor saying hello to the night staff who were just coming on duty. They were talking to the EMI (elderly and mentally infirm) resident named Phyllis who was stark naked except for a long vest.

"Now Phyllis, let's go back to bed shall we" the night staff were saying.

"OK" Phyllis answered "that would be nice."

"Oh well another day in the madhouse over" I said as I left the building.

Chapter 14

Ghosts and 'things that go bump in the night' started to visit our home a couple of years after it was opened, we didn't really take any notice of them until the things that were happening became a little too obvious to ignore and the residents started to see things. We found out that a well-respected gypsy clairvoyant had lived for many years in an old house that had been here before the home was built and that she didn't want to leave so she put a curse upon the ground.

Now as soon as this knowledge was known the more imaginative of our staff started to see things and began to listen to the tales that our residents were telling them. Imagination or not I had a couple of experiences myself and on one occasion I was on my own unit and was asked to go up to the office for something, I can't remember what. It was one of those evening's I don't get very often and was saying to myself as I walked up the corridor.

"Yeah, I feel good and I am at peace with the world." Straight away I could hear a conversation going on between a few women, I couldn't hear the content (probably because working in a home you try not to overhear residents conversation, you tend to switch off) but I felt there was something not quite right, so I backtracked a few steps but to my disappointment there was no one there. Feeling distracted I carried on up the corridor and heard suddenly over my shoulder.

"Aye aye lady"

I turned and heard it again, very plain and aimed directly at me, then nothing. Now if I had been a little more experienced in these matters maybe I could have answered but at the time I was a little unnerved and excited about what had happened. I wanted to tell someone so off I went. I never heard anything like that again and I now have a very open mind about it all.

Our corridor on Beech seemed to be the place that had the most 'happenings', the officers bedroom was on our corridor along with the staff room and kitchen so it was always very busy. The officers had a few 'happenings' that really unnerved them and one officer in particular had refused to sleep in the bedroom at all but it was the night staff that had to pay the consequences. Whenever she was on duty the night staff had to take the mattress off the bed and drag it up to the library and make up a bed for her in there, this went on for years until one of the other officers had had enough. We really didn't mind our ghosts in fact we had names for them, we felt they weren't hurting anyone so left them alone but the office had other ideas so it was on a Friday after dinner that 'he' arrived.

A man of the cloth appeared we don't know where he came from and it was one of the officers that had arranged it all. Here he was all set for the 'exorcism' of the home, some of the staff walked down onto our corridor and tried to warn the ghosts what was going on. Most of us thought it was all very silly and we watched as this chap, with holy water in one hand and a shaker thing in the other, walked up and down the corridor saying something holy. Our officer was walking behind him with a couple of staff being nosey and behind them were two domestics one with a wet mop one with a dry cloth getting the holy water up just in case one of the residents slipped on the wet surface. Even though it was all very silly it seemed to hold a very dark and medieval feeling and the majority of the staff didn't like the whole thing, we felt our ghosts hadn't hurt anyone so why move them on.

A couple of weeks later all of our electrical equipment went down and of course it was all blamed on the exorcist chap. We had to do our entire residents personal washing on the unit (instead of sending it down to the laundry) and of course we had nowhere to dry it. This caused quite a problem with wet washing all over the place steaming up the corridors. Matron was having a fit about it all, until some of the staff took it upon themselves to put up washing lines. They hung all the washing out to dry, which was great until the morning. The washing had been left out all night and when it was brought in it had millions of huge daddy long legs on it (which caused me to have time off with my nerves), why couldn't they have just left the ghosts alone!

My first day back and it had been raining all day so I knew there couldn't be any washing out thank goodness. Sylv was in the bathroom with Vida just finishing off her bath.

"I'm just doing the security check." I called to Sylv.

"Yeah OK, I'll be with you in just a moment." She answered. At that with my mind on my work I held on to the handle of the open window in the kitchen and was just about to close it when the wind pulled the window and me outwards, as I went someone gave me such a slap across the face, I quickly closed the window with a slam causing a resident to shout.

"What the hell's the matter with you?" She asked looking quite concerned.

"I've just been slapped across the face by someone outside." I said, "listen they're still there." The wind seemed to pick up at this point and all we could hear was rustling in the bushes. We were too scared to look out of the window into the dark just in case someone was looking back at us the same moment (if that had happened in my nervous state I would have probably died and that would have been that). Sylv then took charge and holding onto the curtain she quickly pulled it back, thankfully the only thing holding her attention was her own reflection. Then 'SLAP' something hit the window, Sylv almost wet herself as she flew over to phone Matron.

"Yes Matron, we think someone is out there casing the home ready to rob us" said Sylv, she put the phone down "Matron is on her way" she said.

We sat listening to the sounds outside thinking that whoever it was would get a hell of a shock if Matron got to them. Matron came straight down; she didn't bother asking for any explanation, she went straight to the window and pulled the curtain back in one swift movement. It was then that we saw Vida's long legged rain soaked knickers hanging on the line and occasionally slapping at the bushes and window! Matron opened the window, snatched them in and almost threw them at us! She turned and sighed as she walked across the lounge, Sylv just looked at me.

"Well thanks a bloody bunch," she said.

"What did I do?" I said "It wasn't me who phoned Matron, you did that all by yourself."

"You made me look a complete fool." Sylv carried on.

"Yeah well, I looked a fool as well, didn't I?"

"Yeah" said Sylv, "but Matron expects it of you!"

"Oh right" I said as I picked up Vida's knickers "thanks a lot and if she thinks I'm going to wash these she can think again." Then the titters started and we couldn't stop.

"I thought we were goners this time," Sylv said "Did you see Matrons face, blimey I didn't know if she was going to sack us or promote us!"

Chapter 15

Elaine and Kate had been getting along just fine or so we thought, Elaine being on another planet some of the time and Kate just being Kate. So it came as quite a shock when we heard Elaine mumbling around the unit, not so you could hear what she was saying but enough to really annoy the listener. We decided to have a little chat.

"Elaine" I asked "can we have a chat sometime?"

"Why?" Came the short reply.

"Well, we seem to be picking up that you have a worry and we thought that we may be able to help you." I said.

"Oh well" she almost shouted "it's taken you long enough, with me almost going round the bend with tiredness."

"OK" said Sylv "let's go into your room and sort this out." So off the three of us trooped with Elaine taking the lead. She plonked herself down on her bed and we got ready for the onslaught, but it didn't happen, instead she began to cry into her chest. We both looked at each other wondering what on earth was going on.

"Whatever's the matter?" I asked putting my hand on her knee.

"Oh my goodness" she started "I really don't want to do this but I'm getting so tired and was hoping someone would see what was going on before I had to say something." She looked at me and carried on. "It's Kate." Sylv and I heaved a sigh of relief (not that we were guilty of anything but you never know). Elaine went on to say that Kate hadn't been sleeping at night and it was worrying Elaine to death mainly because Kate had taken to getting up and doing her washing (handkerchiefs mainly), then getting dressed and undressed again. Elaine didn't mind that but Kate was so unsteady she was frightened she would have a fall.

"And now just look at her" she shouted "fast asleep in the lounge! I'm just so tired but I can't sleep in the day."

"OK" I said "now don't you worry about it, now that we know what's been going on we'll sort it out."

We went straight to Matron and had a good old moan about the night staff and why they hadn't picked up on it and what do we do now. Matron decided to try and change Kate's sleeping patterns by keeping her awake more during the day. A plan was put into motion and every time we saw Katie asleep we were to gently wake her. Now to Kate we were being right horrible she couldn't understand why she had to stay awake, consequently she started to moan at us then call us all the names under the sun, she didn't care if relatives where there or not.

"Stop tap tap tapping my bloody arm will you" and she would shake her arm very nearly clouting one of us.

This couldn't go on and the Doctor was called, he prescribed sleeping tablets for Kate and they did the trick but unfortunately Kate was also quite drowsy during the day. This made poor Elaine frightened to leave her side because now if Kate decided to get up for anything she was very unsteady and we were all worried she may fall.

Meanwhile a notice went up in reception.

Yoga.

Classes to start Tuesday. Please inform the office if you are interested.

Well Carol, Sylv and I liked this idea, we decided to take a couple of our residents up with us, we had never been to a yoga class in our lives but anything to help relax was fine by us. Elaine would benefit from relaxation and she was mentally alert enough to understand. Vida and Lucy would be asked as well because of their wheelchairs it would be nice for them to join in with something that may suit them, when we asked all concerned they said they were looking forward to it.

Tuesday came and Sylv, Carol and I all with our little mats tucked under our arms chatted to Vida and Lucy about what to expect from the evening.

"Blimey Jackie, I haven't a clue but it's nice to get off the unit and meet a group of youngish normal people for a change."

"Oh yeah" we all agreed.

"Normal is stretching it a bit." Carol said.

We all had a little talk from the lady at the front of the class, she explained how to find your own place in your head somewhere quiet that you can go to for relaxation and meditation. Elaine kept answering as she spoke to the class.

"Oh yes, very true." And "hum I know." The worst was "so can I take myself off for a dirty weekend then." Carol, Slyv and I disowned her at this point and moved closer to Vida and Lucy, we all joined in and near to the end of the class we were told to place our mats on the floor giving us plenty of room to lie without touching anyone else's aura. Sylv took Vida and I took Lucy over to the side wall near the doorway so that they could have a little more space and so could we.

"Ok" the tutor continued "calmly and quietly start to relax you toes...now your feet and ankles...soften them and feel now your body is melting into the floor..." we were really getting into this and the tutor moved over to the lights and switched them off as she carried on talking, taking us up the body relaxing every muscle. It was a little unfortunate that we had to listen to Elaine too who seemed to have missed the plot somewhere and was still in her dirty weekend mode and making all sorts of noises. So, in the almost quiet and almost darkness we could just hear Vida and Lucy mumbling.

"Blimey O'Riley, I can't see a thing are you still there Lucy?"

"I could do with the loo right about now." They carried on. It was about then that all hell broke loose.

"Bloody Hell!" someone shouted followed by what can only be described as a fluttering of papers. Our meditation state was shattered.

"Will someone switch the fecking lights on?" The voice bellowed. Everyone lay still not wanting to come back to this angry noisy place and who could blame us.

"I think my legs gone." Someone said in the dark.

"What the bloody hell is this?"

As the lights went back on we could see Lucy and Vida in fits of laughter as Matron tried desperately to pick up the Doctors notes. They had shot out of his hands when he had tripped, then flew into the darkness landing on top of our Elaine (who thought all her wishes had come at once). At this sight Sylv and I tried to make ourselves invisible, grabbing Vida and Lucy and racing them back onto our unit where our pent up laughter burst from us all in an uncontrolled roar!

After the first Yoga experience Matron laid the rules down and one of them was that on no account was Elaine to go into the Yoga class, we hadn't been told the reason but we all had a fair guess (Elaine had quite a few little illnesses for a few months after that).

The sleeping tablets that had been prescribed for Kate had worked (to a fashion) for a few months and Elaine had managed to regain her sleeping routine but Kate was getting used to the strength of them and they started to have less and less effect. It was the night staff that had brought it to Matrons attention saying that Kate had taken to walking about in the night, frightening them to death on a few occasions. In the end it was decided that Kate was to be moved into the EMI unit for her own safety. Our night staff based themselves on that unit and eventually if Kate was having a wander they would let her sit with them having milky drinks until she was sleepy enough to go back to bed. Consequently she slept most of the day away again. Elaine used to go and visit her and because of Kate's mental state she began to think Elaine was her daughter, Elaine was overjoyed when relatives came and it took years off her so it suited them both.

Now because Elaine was feeling much better about the world she wasn't drinking as much and had decided to take her man friend up on his suggestion of a holiday together. Elaine was full of it, Matron had been in touch with the family on her behalf and they had been quite excited about the whole thing. They had sent Matron holiday money for her and she had brought new holiday clothes in lovely modern colours and John had been very flattering towards her when she had given us all a fashion show. So off they had gone with cases thrown into the back of John's car, both smiling at each other in that 'I know something you don't know' sort of way.

The next morning Matron asked me to stay behind after the morning report. Yet again I could feel my heart beating faster (not that I had done anything wrong I consciously knew about it was just that respect we had for Matron). She generally only asked you to stay behind if there was a problem and she wanted to give you a real telling off in the comfort of her office without anyone overhearing or seeing your embarrassment.

"Yes Matron" I said as I looked about for some sort of help from my colleagues, but none came so in the office I walked.

"Now Jackie, don't look so worried, it's just that recently you requested if any nights came up you'd like to be considered for them, do you still want them?" I was a little off balance by now and would have said yes to anything just to get out of the office and into reception.

"Well yes" I said "I would like to try them"

"Next week Vicky, who is on nights is on holiday and as you know the night staff usually cover their own holidays. We have been asked to use the day staff to cover just in case anyone is needed in the future." Matron then gave me the dates I would be doing and out the office I went. It was only then that I looked at the dates and low and behold it would be the next four Sundays. What a bloody fool I had been to be taken in like this, and by Matron, who I trusted to be fair. Still I had accepted them and there was nothing I could do about it (make the best of it Matron, I thought because I wouldn't be this daft again). I felt at this point that my world had caved in Matron wasn't the fair person I thought her to be and this came as quite a shock, I felt as though I was being laughed at and began to have my first taste of stress related anxiety I really didn't like it, but plod on I did.

The night shifts came and on the third Sunday I was working with Kath, she was Irish and just the best person in the world. With that typical Irish outspoken way chatting about everything under the sun we had a great shift, I found my worst time was about three in the morning just when the birds were waking and the foxes were making their way home after scavenging around the bushes and bins.

Kath had been working nights for ages and it was her way of life. It meant that you have one to one care with the residents from toileting to dying and everything that came in between, so you would have quiet nights then very busy nights. I was still very much a newcomer to this rewarding one to one care so when Kath asked me to just pop down to the laundry and get some dry sheets off I went, but a little nervous in this half-light of night. The noises in the night seem to heighten your senses until you can hear a foot fall anywhere in the home and locate it to the nearest inch. So as I walked very quietly past the officer's bedroom I heard a noise, now it wasn't a normal night time noise, it sounded like a loud clapping sound and it was getting nearer. Frozen, I couldn't move, I wanted to run but all I could do was lean on the officers door and tap it with my nails mainly because that was all I could move by now with this 'clap, clap, clap' coming in rhythm now. It was about then that the officer called.

"What, what's the matter?" as they roused out of their sleep, I could hear Kathy coming down the other corridor calling as quietly as she could.

"Jackie. It's OK." But it was too late the officer was awake and popping hear head out from behind the door just as we could see Kate trying to run down the corridor totally in the nip! The clapping we could now all hear came from her rather large bosoms slapping her tummy as she half ran!

I will never forget that sight half funny, half so very sad. Poor Kate had been worried and had come looking for us. Kath had been in the middle of the two hourly report and hadn't noticed she had gone until it was too late and I had never heard anything like that before but it did make me realise nights weren't for me, it was a little too quiet.

Kate didn't make Christmas that year and I had had my eyes opened about some of the officers and their 'couldn't give a damn' attitude towards the staff but with that came my fight back future and my new responsibilities as Union Steward.